EUROPE

- ● **AFRICA**
- ● **ASIA**
- ● **AUSTRALIA**
- **EUROPE**
- ● **NORTH AMERICA**
- ● **CENTRAL AMERICA**
- **SOUTH AMERICA**
- ❶ **PAGE NUMBER OF LOCATION**

EUROPE

AFRICA

ASIA

AUSTRALIA

87
65
26
36
68
66
126
24 59
27
53 The Bosporus
108
104 Jerusalem
Cairo 109
amel
98 The Forbidden City
125 Kyoto
The Huangshan Mountains 60 43 Nanjing
76 The Sun Kosi River
Wildflower Hall 122
Rajasthan 34
116 Vietnam
Phuket by Elephant 49
88 Palau
50 The Masai Mara
54 Borneo's Rainforests
Cape Town 106
33 Sydney Opera House
The Tongariro Northern Circuit 84
Lake Wanaka 134

DREAM
Destinations

100 of the World's Best Vacations

The Sahara Desert, Morocco

The Huangshan Mountains, China

Dream
Destinations

LIFE Books

EDITOR Robert Sullivan
DIRECTOR OF PHOTOGRAPHY Barbara Baker Burrows
CREATIVE DIRECTOR Richard Baker
DEPUTY PICTURE EDITOR Christina Lieberman
WRITER-REPORTER Hildegard Anderson
COPY Barbara Gogan (Chief), Parlan McGaw
CONSULTING PICTURE EDITORS
Mimi Murphy (Rome), Tala Skari (Paris)

Special thanks to Doug Look

PRESIDENT Andrew Blau
BUSINESS MANAGER Roger Adler
BUSINESS DEVELOPMENT MANAGER Jeff Burak

EDITORIAL OPERATIONS Richard K. Prue,
David Sloan (Directors), Richard Shaffer
(Group Manager), Brian Fellows, Raphael Joa,
Angel Mass, Stanley E. Moyse, Albert Rufino
(Managers), Soheila Asayesh, Keith Aurelio,
Trang Ba Chuong, Charlotte Coco, Osmar Escalona,
Kevin Hart, Norma Jones, Mert Kerimoglu,
Rosalie Khan, Marco Lau, Po Fung Ng, Rudi Papiri,
Barry Pribula, Carina A. Rosario, Christopher Scala,
Diana Suryakusuma, Vaune Trachtman,
Paul Tupay, Lionel Vargas, David Weiner

Time Inc. Home Entertainment
PUBLISHER Richard Fraiman
GENERAL MANAGER Steven Sandonato
EXECUTIVE DIRECTOR, MARKETING SERVICES Carol Pittard
DIRECTOR, RETAIL & SPECIAL SALES Tom Mifsud
DIRECTOR, NEW PRODUCT DEVELOPMENT Peter Harper
ASSISTANT DIRECTOR, BRAND MARKETING Laura Adam
ASSOCIATE COUNSEL Helen Wan
BOOK PRODUCTION MANAGER Suzanne Janso
DESIGN & PREPRESS MANAGER Anne-Michelle Gallero
SENIOR MARKETING MANAGER Joy Butts
ASSOCIATE BRAND MANAGER Shelley Rescober

Special thanks to Alexandra Bliss,
Glenn Buonocore, Susan Chodakiewicz,
Robert Marasco, Brooke Reger, Mary Sarro-Waite,
Ilene Schreider, Adriana Tierno, Alex Voznesenskiy

Copyright 2008 Time Inc. Home Entertainment

Published by **LIFE Books**

Time Inc.
1271 Avenue of the Americas
New York, NY 10020

ISBN 10: 1-60320-010-X
ISBN 13: 978-1-60320-010-3
Library of Congress #: 2007910089

"LIFE" is a trademark of Time Inc.

We welcome your comments and suggestions about
LIFE Books. Please write to us at:
LIFE Books
Attention: Book Editors
PO Box 11016
Des Moines, IA 50336-1016

If you would like to order any of our hardcover
Collector's Edition books,
please call us at 1-800-327-6388
(Monday through Friday, 7:00 a.m.–8:00 p.m.,
or Saturday, 7:00 a.m.–6:00 p.m., Central Time).

Printed in Mexico

CONTENTS

Peggy's Cove, Nova Scotia

GERALD BRIMACOMBE

Come, Journey with Us

MADISON JULIUS CAWEIN—"The Keats of Kentucky"—was a well-known poet at the turn of the 20th century who is largely forgotten today. For his "Song of the Road," he composed a bit of verse that sets a nice tone as we venture forth to some of the world's most delightful places to vacation:

> Again let us dream where the land lies sunny
> And live, like the bees, on our hearts' old honey,
> Away from the world that slaves for money—
> Come, journey the way with me.

Yes, indeed, let's leave behind the day job, the world that slaves for money, and let us dream of these places where the land lies sunny. That's what we at LIFE hope to allow you to do—in these pages and, perhaps, in real life.

This is a book of inspiration and aspiration. Some of the places herein exalt the spirit simply by their exquisite natural beauty:

The sublimity of a forest in Bucks County, Pennsylvania, in autumn can't be topped, unless, of course, by the startling clarity of the springtime light on Lake Wanaka in New Zealand . Nor can the Alpine grandeur of China's Huangshan Mountains be beat, unless you trump it with that old American standby, Yosemite.

Never heard of Wanaka or the Huangshans? Good, then our book is already succeeding. *Dream Destinations* could easily have become a rundown of a hundred usual suspects. And though some of those are represented here, to be sure, we have tried to select surprises, even secrets. Have you ever heard of The Point? Well, take it from us, you may have already booked your room, but you've got a ways to go before you find the place. And when we do go for the tried-and-true, such as Yosemite, we approach it from an unfamiliar angle (in this instance, through the doors of the park's grand and gorgeous Ahwahnee Hotel).

Yes, some of these places are inspiring in and of themselves, and seeing them rendered in pictures may give you a quiet thrill. We

Where does your dream lie? Is it in the exotic lushness of the Mekong Delta in Vietnam (opposite)? Or just beneath the surface of the sea in the Bahamas (above)? Or perhaps on the links along the Oregon coast (left). They're all yours for the dreaming.

hope this might lead to a second kind of inspiration, one where you are moved to not only add them to your life list of places to visit but to actually get up off that couch and go. People have vastly different interests, we know that, and so our dream destinations have been organized in categories: those that are especially family friendly, those that may appeal to the energetic, those of interest to culture vultures and so on. All would enjoy reading about any one of these sites, but if you're seeking something specific to your own desires, then this is the place for you.

THE WRITER ANAÏS NIN once observed, "Dreams are necessary to life," and this brings us to aspiration. We have included in each of our six categories an impossible dream. You may not want to bungee jump off a bridge at Victoria Falls, but you might well want to see what that looks like, and wonder if, in your superhero daydreams, you could take the plunge. You may think you don't have the chops to play at Carnegie Hall, but did you know that maybe, just maybe, you could? The impossible dreams are out-there vacations only the most out-there among us might aspire to. But they're great fun for all of us to contemplate.

Similarly, some of the other dream destinations in this book could be beyond our means. The islands of the South Pacific might be too far away, and this inn or that one may simply be too dear. In these instances, please consider our book as a service. We'll give you destinations to dream about, and we'll leave it at that. Dreams—aspirations—are necessary to life. They keep us optimistic and looking forward to the future. Maybe one day . . .

So here we go, to a hundred of the very best places to holiday in the world. We'll travel under the waves and up to the top of mountains, to a real-world Shangri-La, to great cities and all-but-secret villages. We will venture into the realm of the Medicis and of Dracula and of George Washington. We will voyage in search of lost Atlantis and of bygone dinosaurs. And we'll travel the world—first seated in our armchairs with this book, and then . . . well, that's up to you.

FOR FAMILIES ▶

London

ENGLAND'S GREAT CITY is fascinating, of course, but it's also great fun. A family with older children will thrill as school lessons come alive at Shakespeare's Globe Theatre and as history is relived on walking tours themed after everything from Charles Dickens novels to the gruesome doings of Jack the Ripper. Take a spin on the ultramodern Millennium Wheel (seen here with good old Big Ben, right, and the Houses of Parliament in the background). The Science Museum is as interactive as a playground, the Museum of Natural History is not to be missed, and the British Museum is nonpareil; best of all, most museums are free, which is a boon these days when the dollar is so outweighed by Britain's currency, the pound. Londoners speak our language, more or less, and any American kid will delight when he or she learns that an "English breakfast" is a repast fit for Falstaff, while late afternoon "high tea" really translates as "dessert"—and lots of it.

Riviera Maya

FAR FROM ITS FAMOUS French namesake is a seaside paradise more than 50 miles long that attracts not the glitterati in pursuit of glamour but families seeking fun and adventure. Mexico's Riviera Maya, which stretches down the Yucatán Peninsula, features snow-white beaches and, just offshore in the warm waters of the Caribbean Sea, the second-largest barrier coral reef in the world. There is exotic swimming inland, too, in the cenotes—deep natural pools of crystal-clear water connected to underground rivers. The Mayans of yore thought the cenotes led to the underworld, but to the present-day tourist they represent portals to paradise. Older children will be fascinated by the Mayan ruins at Tulum (El Castillo looks down upon the ocean from atop a dramatic cliff) and Coba; and all ages will be awed by the giant caves of Aktun Chen, where stalactites and stalagmites grow in caverns beneath a thriving rainforest.

19° 30' N, 99° 10' W

ALEX WEBB/MAGNUM

Orlando

BEGINNING IN 1971, when the first turnstile was turned at Walt Disney World's Magic Kingdom, a gleaming city has bloomed in erstwhile Florida citrus groves. As we know, that city stands now as an unparalleled entertainment mecca beckoning the world's children. The Disney universe here has grown far beyond the boundaries of Main Street U.S.A.—Animal Kingdom is a must-visit, as is Hollywood Studios (above); Splash Mountain is a world-class water park; and several of the Disney hotels now boast five-star dining. But Orlando is, today, much more than just Disney. Yes, there are the other theme parks, such as Universal Studios and SeaWorld, but believe us: There's even more. Golf fit for Tiger (he lives here, by the way) is plentiful, and on Florida's nearby eastern shore are beaches worthy of the French or Mexican Riviera. Take in an Orlando Magic basketball game, or tour NASA's Kennedy Space Center. Once just a gleam in Walt Disney's eye, Orlando is now a magical, multidimensional trip for any family.

28° 32' N, 81° 22' W

Wisconsin Dells

A CENTURY AND A HALF AGO when folks living along this meandering stretch of the Wisconsin River got into the tourist business, they could not possibly have envisioned *this*. These days the Dells bills itself as the Waterpark Capital of the World, and the boast is hard to refute. To be sure, this particular dream destination might seem nightmarish to some, but a quick rundown of the Dells' charms will let any reader know if it is the place for them. There are 200 waterslides, surf-wave pools and lazy rivers in nearly two dozen separate indoor and outdoor water parks. Other amusement parks feature ferocious roller coasters and go-kart racing. The Dells has attractions with names such as Halley's Comet Racers and Poseidon's Rage, a theater offering movies in "4-D" and resorts that brag of their "Huge Themed Fantasy Suites." *Whew!* Long ago, fishing and floating were what attracted visitors (and do still, among some folks, as the picture below proves). When measured against the neighboring reality, though, scenes such as this seem . . . quaint.

PETER DASILVA/THE NEW YORK TIMES/REDUX

GERALD BRIMACOMBE

THE AHWAHNEE NATIVE AMERICANS who lived in these spectacular mountains and valleys in central California bequeathed the name of what is today one of the world's most stunning national parks: Yosemite, meaning grizzly bear. They also quite inadvertently lent their own tribal moniker to what would become one of the country's grandest inns, Yosemite's rustic but elegant Ahwahnee Hotel. The hotel—not to mention the park—is wonderful in summer, but perhaps even more wondrous in winter; a highlight since its opening in 1927 has been the annual Christmas-season Bracebridge Dinners, replete with all the Old English trappings.

The Ahwahnee Hotel

A second fine option in Yosemite, particularly for families on a budget, is Housekeeping Camp, right down by the banks of the Merced River. There are 266 cabins here; each sleeps up to six. You, too, have the millionaire's views of the awesome, ponderous summit of Half Dome; of majestic Yosemite Falls, a cascade of water 2,425 feet long, which makes it the highest waterfall in North America. Greet the dawn and then go exploring. The hikes are as good as it gets, and the signature sights—such as the sheer face of El Capitan, the world's largest granite rock (twice as big as Gibraltar)—will create memories to last a lifetime.

New York City

THE SKATING RINK at Rockefeller Center and the Christmas Spectacular at Radio City Music Hall . . . the Bronx Zoo and, across the street, the New York Botanical Garden . . . the Metropolitan Museum of Art and the Modern . . . the Public Library and, in Greenwich Village, the Strand ("18 Miles of new, used, rare and out-of-print books") . . . Yankee Stadium in the Bronx and Shea over in Queens . . . a spin on the carousel in Central Park (above), and maybe a row across the lake . . . Carnegie Hall and the Brooklyn Academy of Music . . . Ellis Island and the Statue of Liberty . . . the Empire State Building and the ceiling in Grand Central Terminal . . . the American Museum of Natural History . . . Broadway, with everything from the Bard to Disney, and off-Broadway and off-off-Broadway . . . the finest dining anywhere and, not least, much of the very best pizza: This is New York City, family-style.

40°42′ N, 74°0′ W

The Bahamas

24° 15'N, 76°0' W

THESE SHIMMERING ISLANDS in the Atlantic Ocean used to be considered a playground for adults. There were casinos and nightclubs and honeymoon specials galore—and, certainly, there still are. But in recent years, some of the world's most sensational family-friendly resorts have been built here, and the Bahamas have become a magnet for vacationers of any age. Cable Beach might be the finest on the island of Nassau, and on what used to be a very quiet stretch of white sand, there now frolic children whose families are guests at the SuperClubs Breezes resort. Over on Grand Bahama Island, daily activities, from snorkeling tours to para-sailing trips, are organized at the Our Lucaya resort. And on Paradise Island is Atlantis: In this universe unto itself are slot machines for the oldsters, outrageous waterslides for the youngsters and miles of white sand beach for everyone. There is golf, from mini to maxi. Winding throughout is the largest man-made marine habitat in the world, where sharks and other fish (such as this sawfish, below) swim by on the other side of the glass as Junior floats on his tube, or as Mom digs into her grouper filet in an undersea restaurant (one of the resort's 17 eateries). Atlantis was, legendarily, a lost utopia. It is found.

GAIL MOONEY/CORBIS

DONALD NAUSBAUM/CORBIS

Snowmass

THE ARGUMENT CAN BE MADE that there is nothing so warming for a family as a ski vacation. The first summit with Dad or Mom, the last run as dusk settles in, the hot chocolate and hot-tub afterglow: They all serve to draw us together in a cozy winter huddle. Many ski resorts celebrate what the sport and its accoutrements mean to a family. In the East you have Maine's Sunday River, New Hampshire's Bretton Woods and Vermont's Okemo and Smuggler's Notch, each of which has a richly deserved reputation as a family-friendly outpost. In the West, there are Montana's Big Sky, Utah's Deer Valley and Colorado's Keystone and Beaver Creek. Also in the Centennial State is Snowmass—the second largest ski area in the country, with the very highest vertical rise (4,406 feet), but at heart a gentle giant. It is in Aspen, yes, but it does not represent the Aspen you might think of. It is less about movie stars and more about a brilliantly star-filled night. Less about steeps (though it has plenty) and more about the Elk Camp Meadows learning area, with its new gondola for getting the kids there quick. It is about the family joined around an evening fire.

Memphis

WHEN YOU CONSIDER Memphis, what do you conjure? The mighty Mississippi, which brought the city into being? The music and the phenomenal Elvis, who stamped his presence here and who lives on eternally? The epochal assassination that took place in 1968, sending aftershocks throughout the nation that are still felt today? All these are commemorated effectively in Memphis, making it a destination for families with teens who are hip or smart or, praise be, both. Visit the Rock 'n' Soul Museum and the Stax Museum of American Soul Music, and learn that Memphis has always been about much more than rock 'n' roll. Or go to a club on Beale Street (below) and hear the real thing. By all means, pay homage to "the Pelvis" at Sun Studios and at Graceland, where he lived, now a National Historic Landmark. Relax on a riverboat on the Mississippi, channeling Mark Twain. Drop by the Peabody Hotel at 11 a.m. for the daily Duck Parade, during which five ducks kept in pens on the roof emerge from the elevator, march across a red carpet and splash into the hotel's fountain. And do not miss the National Civil Rights Museum, which recounts the history of our nation's seminal struggle. Visit the Lorraine Motel where Martin Luther King Jr. was gunned down. Let the moment resonate.

KEVIN FLEMING/CORBIS

35° 8' N, 90° 3' W

Cuzco

CALL THESE THE VACATIONS of the Samaritans or, perhaps, Altruists on Holiday. They are a new way for a person to think about what to put into his or her time off, and what reward he or she expects to take away from that experience. The concept: Individuals or groups, including in many instances families, volunteer to go to a place where aid is needed and, for a week or more, pitch in. Habitat for Humanity sponsors such efforts throughout the world (minimum age, 16), but there are many other organizations as well. On the American Hiking Society's Volunteer Vacations, participants rebuild footpaths and shelters as they trek. The Global Citizens Network aids 83 villages (370,000 people) in the poorest regions of Tanzania in Africa. In South America, the ancient city of Cuzco is alternately known as the Heart of the Incan Empire or as the gateway to one of the world's great wonders, the ruins of the Incan citadel Machu Picchu—but there is much poverty. The organization Globe Aware, which runs volunteer vacations in other countries, too, has two sites in Cuzco where tourists work with needy children in promoting self-esteem, learning about hygiene and even developing work skills. Games are played, songs are sung and crafts are made—and, of course, the surrounding Peruvian attractions are visited (opposite, the rail line taking travelers from Cuzco up to Machu Picchu). The vacationer is enriched in many ways.

13°9'S, 72°32'W

Montana's Dude Ranches

OUTDOORS IN THE BIG SKY COUNTRY, where the range extends gloriously to majestic mountains beyond, everybody feels like a cowboy or cowgirl: You just want to saddle up and ride. Throughout Montana, at dozens of dude ranches small and large, you can—and you can hike, fish, hunt, picnic, mountain bike or play a game of horseshoes. In winter, you can draw up to the campfire at the 320 Guest Ranch near West Yellowstone National Park; it's one of the larger establishments (with accommodations for 250 in handsome, comfortable cabins and log homes) and one that courts families with kids of all ages. The 320 is authentic, possessing a heritage dating to when the West was the West. Sam Wilson built his homestead cabin, which still exists on the property, along the Gallatin River in 1898, and shortly thereafter opened the Buffalo Horn Resort. Back in the day, activities didn't include volleyball and whitewater rafting in summer, snowmobiling, sleigh rides and skiing in winter—but they do now.

BRIAN SMITH/CORBIS OUTLINE

Space

IT'S THE RARE KID who hasn't dreamed of being an astronaut. If the British entrepreneur Richard Branson (left) has his way, such dreams could come true in a couple of years. His Burt Rutan–designed line of spaceships are being developed apace, and if safety standards are achieved and government approvals met, there could be space tourism by 2010—or so Sir Richard hopes. Tickets for the first flights may cost as much as $200,000, but the good news is that Virgin Galactic is accepting frequent-flyer "Space Miles" from Branson's Virgin Airlines, and already more than two dozen folks have chalked up enough to take a trip into space. While they wait for the opportunity, they can always attend a space camp, such as this one in Huntsville, Alabama, where astronaut wannabes enjoy a simulated experience that is out of this world.

RICHARD T. NOWITZ (2)

The Uffizi Gallery

This entry might as well be titled "Florence," for indeed the city as a whole stands as one of the artistic wonders of the world. In the Academy Gallery, you'll find Michelangelo's *David* and many other treasures, and then there is the National Museum. But we insist upon the Uffizi Gallery here. Just in case the routinely long lines to get in are encouraging you to give it a pass during your next sojourn in Italy, book tickets in advance for a shorter wait, then get thee to the Uffizi. It was built in the 16th century to house the offices and collections of the Medicis and has been open to the public since 1765. The paintings—among them masterworks by Raphael, Titian, Caravaggio and, of course, Michelangelo—are certainly sensational, but the building itself is no less impressive. To walk beneath stunning ceiling paintings and through the courtyard between the two wings (seen here) is to be overawed by the luxurious aesthetic of the Medicis. If you feel like cleansing your psychic palate after digesting the Uffizi, take a trip into the countryside and walk amidst olive trees in the Tuscan sun.

43° 46′ N, 11° 15′ W •

The State Hermitage Museum

BUILT IN THE MID-18TH CENTURY, the famed Winter Palace in St. Petersburg used to be the grandiose residence of the Russian czars. It is now the lead building among six on the embankment of the River Neva that are home to the some three million works of art. When Catherine the Great began this collection in 1764 with the acquisition of more than 225 paintings, she called her gallery "my hermitage"—and allowed few to share in its splendor: "Only the mice and I can admire all this." Catherine's successor rulers in Russia expanded the collection, scooping up old masters from throughout Europe (the Hermitage eventually had more Rembrandts than any museum), ancient artifacts from the excavations at Troy—anything grand from anywhere at all. After the Russian Revolution of 1917, the Soviet state claimed the burgeoning imperial Hermitage and in the 1920s and '30s, sold off hundreds of "bourgeois" artworks, such as Botticelli's *Adoration of the Magi* and Raphael's *Alba Madonna*. The thinking that led to the sale has long since been reversed, and today the State Hermitage is one of the world's premier museums. You may have been to the Louvre and the British Museum and trod the galleries of Florence, but you haven't seen it all until you've visited the Hermitage.

ART RESOURCE

SUSY MEZZANOTTE/CORBIS

The Vatican Museums

IN A ROMAN VINEYARD IN 1506, a monumental statue of Laocoon, a great priest in Greek mythology, was discovered near where the emperor Nero once lived. Pope Julius II heard of the find and sent two artists who were working at the Vatican—one of whom was Michelangelo Buonarroti—to examine the statue. They reported to the Pope that it was a masterpiece and that he should buy it from the vineyard owner. He did, and thus were the Vatican Museums born. The artistic holdings of the Roman Catholic Church are among the world's most extensive and fabulous and are on display in dozens of galleries in various museums within Vatican City. The Vatican Library, which includes the Sistine Hall (above) contains not only manuscripts but hundreds of thousands of medals, coins, prints and engravings. Items from ancient Egypt, including the *Book of the Dead,* are housed in the Museo Egiziano. In the Museo Pio-Clementino, there are 53 galleries of Greek and Roman sculpture to pass through before arriving at the transcendental Sistine Chapel. Michelangelo is represented everywhere throughout the Vatican, but his ceiling is a masterwork beyond comprehension. The secular as well as the religious cannot help but be moved by its majesty.

Sundance

MORE THAN AN ANNUAL FILM FESTIVAL, more than an institute that sponsors the festival and other cultural enterprises in Utah, more than another Rocky Mountain ski resort, Sundance is a state of mind—specifically the mind of movie star and film director Robert Redford, who gained fame as the Sundance Kid opposite Paul Newman's Butch Cassidy, and who is the godfather of all things Sundance. Redford, an environmentalist and expert skier, founded the resort on spectacular Mount Timpanogos outside Park City in 1969 and set about creating the Sundance experience, an aspirational "perfect blend of art, nature and recreation." The ski area remains rustic, relatively minimalist, and afford- able; visitors tired of the slopes can take a class in painting, pottery or jewelry-making at the Art Shack. Redford was the chairperson of the first Utah/U.S. Film Festival in 1978, which has evolved into Sundance, the largest independent cine-fest in the United States. Go to Utah in January, take in a dozen cutting-edge films, listen to free live music on Park City's Main Street, work on your life list of celeb sightings, glimpse Mr. Redford ("Bob," to many), plunge into the powdery bowls above the resort.... And revel in the blissful Sundance state of mind.

40° 38' N, 111° 29' W

Austin

AN ACTIVIST GROUP IN THIS TEXAS CITY has begun a semi-official movement whose credo is "Keep Austin Weird." Well, there is probably no town in the nation with a weirder confluence of communities and constituencies, each of them appearing profoundly odd to the others. First, there are the pols: Austin being the capital of a huge state, the business of that state is obviously dominant on the scene, with a lot of serious-looking dark-suited folks scurrying about. The city is also home to Dell computers, which has created a kind of sun-baked Silicon Valley atmosphere for its thousands of employees: no neckties, somewhat geeky, very smart. And then you have the cultural Austin, which is to say, its music (not to disregard the museums and theaters). Whereas Nashville is all about country, musical Austin embraces all comers: singer-songwriters, rockers, bluesmen. There's an enormous bronze statue down by the lake that you might think would be of some Alamo hero but in fact depicts local guitar god Stevie Ray Vaughn, who died way too young. The PBS television show *Austin City Limits* showcases the music for a national audience, and the annual South by Southwest music festival has become the Sundance of "alt"—alternative country, alternative rock, alternative anything. Take a stroll down 6th Street, Austin's version of Bourbon Street in New Orleans and listen to the music pour forth on a hot Saturday night. Every Saturday night is hot in weird old Austin.

The Glastonbury Festival

THIS SMALL TOWN of 9,000 souls in Somerset, England, grows like Woodstock did (precisely like Woodstock, in fact, and we'll get to that) during the annual Glastonbury Festival. Before we discuss the music, some history, for there is plenty of it—or at least legend. It is believed by many that within decades of the death of Jesus, Joseph of Arimathea constructed at Glastonbury the country's first Christian church and also hid the Holy Grail somewhere in town. One storied figure who was later involved with the Grail, King Arthur, had many doings in Glastonbury, it is said, and may have been buried in the abbey (which, in its ruined state, remains awe-inspiring). Glastonbury attracts religious pilgrims and Arthurian scholars and for a few days each year, hordes of rock fans. Every June, one of the world's biggest popular music festivals encamps here, and more than 150,000 fans bear down on Somerset. Paul McCartney has headlined, and so have Oasis and Amy Winehouse. As to how the Glastonbury Festival resembles Woodstock: The big bash is actually staged in the nearby, far less famous village of Pilton, just as the original Woodstock extravaganza was, in fact, held in the adjacent town of Bethel, New York. One more Glastonbury legend.

Stratford-upon-Avon

BRUSH UP YOUR SHAKESPEARE here—as nowhere else. This charming English town of 20,000 citizens is thoroughly engaged in the business of preserving, protecting and defending the legacy of its favorite son. William Shakespeare was born in 1564 in his family's farmhouse on Henley Street—now a major shopping and entertainment thoroughfare for Stratford's 3 million annual tourists. The Tudor house has been preserved and is one of several Shakespeare-related buildings that can be toured. These also include the family cottage of Shakespeare's wife, Anne Hathaway, and the house where their daughter resided with her husband. Above is the site where the house that Will lived in for the last few years of his life once stood, and where he died in 1616. He is buried in Stratford's Holy Trinity Church, and visitors pay homage there. You can also attend a West End–quality theatrical production at the Royal Shakespeare Company's 1,000-seat Courtyard Theatre. After the play, enjoy a drink at the Dirty Duck pub and rub elbows with the actors. The evening might not be as raucous as when bad boys Richard Burton and Peter O'Toole raised a pint to the bard during their Stratford residencies, but it will be sufficiently lively. Of that you can be sure.

Hemingway's Havana

HE LIVED IN CUBA ON AND OFF from the 1930s to 1960, working on, among other novels, *For Whom the Bell Tolls, To Have and Have Not, Islands in the Stream* and *The Old Man and the Sea*. He drank in bars that are still in business, imbibing mojitos at La Bodeguita and daiquiris at La Floridita in Hemingwayesque quantities. Yes, certainly: The prerevolution Havana that Ernest Hemingway knew is difficult to sense now, as the once singing city is tattered at best and utterly downcast in many places. But it remains lovely at heart, the people warm and friendly. The author is commemorated in a set-aside room on the fifth floor of the Hotel Ambos Mundos, where he resided and where his typewriter, books and photographs are on display. In 1939, he moved from the hotel to Finca Vigía, or Lookout Farm, a few miles outside the city. This abode, too, can be visited; in fact, it is a museum in Hemingway's honor, with 8,000 of his books shelved as they were when he roamed these rooms and bottles just waiting for Papa (above). When you look to the sea through the same window he did when conjuring the adventure of his hero Santiago, you can feel Hemingway's ghost.

MARC DEVILLE/GAMMA/ZUMA

23° 8′ N, 82° 23′ W

34° 0′ S, 151° 0′ E

Sydney Opera House

THIS GLEAMING JEWEL of Australia's glittering Oz of a city, the Sydney Opera House has been regarded as one of the world's great modern architectural specimens since it opened in 1973, following decades of wrangling, controversy, setbacks, and all other manner of Sturm und Drang. The man who won the commission to design the edifice in 1957, the Dane Jørn Utzon, resigned in 1966, although he'd relocated his entire practice to Australia to oversee the storm-tossed project. The Opera House was finally completed a full decade after the original projection date, with a budget overrun of 1,400 percent ($102 million eventually spent after an initial estimated cost of $7 million) and it was deemed a smashing success. Most striking were the "sails": gigantic precast concrete shells that seem to leap from Sydney Harbor like gamboling whales or dolphins. Their million-plus tiles, shining white in the Down Under sun, gave the antipodes a contemporary face, a signature, a world-class identity. Pictures don't do justice to the immensity of the Opera House, which has two main halls, five theaters and an equal number of rehearsal studios, plus four restaurants and six bars, in its four and a half acres of space. Its energy supply could power a town of 25,000 people. As it is, it fuels Australia's national pride.

LAURIE CHAMBERLAIN/CORBIS

27° 42′ N, 75° 33′ E

Rajasthan

THE CULTURAL ATTRACTIONS of India are, to say the least, vital and exhilarating—and throughout Rajasthan, the largest state in the nation, they are brilliantly on display. Dramatic forts and beautiful temples are to be found in the capital city of Jaipur and in the surrounding countryside as well. It seems someone is always celebrating something in Rajasthan: It is a land of fairs and festivals. Among the largest of dozens of pageants are the Desert

Festival (Rajasthan encompasses most of the Great Indian Desert), the Pushkar Fair, the Elephant Festival and the Camel Festival. Animals are not relegated to the last two, they star at all of the festivals, where they race, perform, give rides and even participate in thrilling polo matches. The city of Udaipur must be visited for its palaces, gardens, mountain views and lakes; it has been called the Venice of the East. If you have the means, stay at the Taj Lake Palace Hotel, an extraordinary all-marble edifice built upon a four-acre island in Lake Pichola (above). The history and culture of modern India has its roots in traditions dating back nearly 5,000 years. In Rajasthan, the past and present meet.

The Musikverein

VIENNA IS THE WORLD CAPITAL of music. Any city that lists Haydn, Mozart, Beethoven, Schubert, the Strausses, Brahms, Schönberg and the alumni of the Vienna Boys Choir among its favorite sons has an indisputable claim. In residence at present, you have the Vienna Philharmonic Orchestra, the Vienna Symphony Orchestra, the Vienna Volksoper Symphony Orchestra, the Vienna Radio Symphony Orchestra, the Vienna Chamber Orchestra, the Jeunesse, the Gustav Mahler Jugendorchester and the Pierrot Lunaire Ensemble Vienna—not to mention the eternal Boys Choir, hitting high notes since 1498. These ensembles make heavenly sounds in a half-dozen splendid concert halls and opera houses throughout the city. We cite here the Musikverein ("music club"), which opened in 1870 and is considered to have one of the three great acoustical auditoriums in the world (the others being Boston's Symphony Hall and Amsterdam's Concertgebouw). Up to 500 concerts are staged yearly in the Musikverein's five auditoriums—the Golden Hall is its most famous room, not least for the joyous annual New Year's concert by the Philharmonic (below), which draws devotees from around the world.

HANS PUNZ/AP

48° 14' N, 16° 20' E

The Liceu

BARCELONA IS A CITY OF PASSION, and La Rambla, the storied boulevard that inspires a nightly promenade of Barcelonans, is, if such a thing can be imagined, a passionate street. Its cafes are ablaze till dawn; song is constantly in the air. From the moment the Gran Teatre del Liceu opened there, on April 4, 1847, it was clear that it belonged on La Rambla. Opera is, by definition, a passionate art form and only profits from a grandiose setting. The Liceu's auditorium is enormous, ornate and simply stunning.

Balconies rise five tiers; the cheap seats in the *galliner* ("hen roost") are usually filled with true opera buffs who are happy to shower both praise and derision from on high. The Liceu has seen great drama on its stage and in its own history. In 1861, the building was damaged, and in 1994, it was virtually destroyed by fire. In 1893, on an opening night, 22 patrons were killed by an anarchist's bomb. Legendary conductors (Stravinsky, Toscanini) have worked here, as have singers from Callas to Pavarotti, each of them dispensing passion to rapt Catalan audiences. Milan's La Scala, London's Covent Garden and New York's Metropolitan Opera House are going to be on any opera lover's must-see list, but a night at the Liceu is like none other.

41°23′N, 2°9′E

Gauguin's Tahiti

THE FRENCH postimpressionist Paul Gauguin's years in Tahiti represented a quest, an effort to bring something new to painting while investigating the life and mythology of native Polynesians: "Through arrangements of lines and colors, I get symphonies and harmonies representing nothing truly real in the vulgar sense of the word, expressing directly no idea, but like music makes you think, without the help of ideas or images, simply through those mysterious affinities that are behind our brains." The dozens of canvases he produced here sparked some interest back in Paris—where painters such as Degas were taken by Gauguin's fresh use of color—but brought Gauguin neither fame nor fortune. The paintings, now recognized to be masterpieces, in no way reflect how fraught Gauguin's stay in Polynesia often was; by the time he was nearing his death in the Marquesas in 1903 at age 54, he was diseased, impoverished, a morphine user, sometimes suicidal and in trouble with the law. So then: how to approach Gauguin's Tahiti today? Do not go looking for enjoyable tributes to the painter equivalent of Monet's gardens at Giverny. There is a Gauguin Museum, but it's more about the man than the art and owns none of his original paintings. Rather, drive out into the rural areas, walk the black sand beaches, contemplate the waterfalls, sit under the banyan tree, try to find what he was trying to find: "Over there, in the silence of tropical nights, I will be able to listen to the soft music whispering the motions from my heart."

FARRELL GREHAN/CORBIS

MARTIN KERS/GETTY

Giverny

49°4'N, 1°31'E

YOU KNOW THIS PLACE even if you've never visited. At the very least, you know its most famous gardens. Giverny is an old village about 50 miles west of Paris. In 1883, it was a charming hamlet of perhaps 300 citizens, clustered around a small stone church that dated to the Middle Ages. It was in that year that the painter Claude Monet passed by in a train, and fell in love. He soon rented a house in town, a property he later bought. Giverny back then, small though it was, boasted a thriving artistic community, with many impressionist painters, several of them Americans, in residence. Monet would become their hero. At his house, he built and grew the things he wished to paint: a water lily pond (above), a Japanese bridge, the Grand Allee, the famous flower garden. His luminescent, moving pictures of scenes from his own backyard contributed to his renown, and are considered masterworks. Monet died in Giverny in 1926 and was buried in the village cemetery. His property languished through decades of disuse before it was renovated and opened to the public in 1980. Each year, it draws a multitude of art aficionados, who also visit the American Art Museum a hundred yards away. Then they repair to the cafe at the Hôtel Baudy for a restorative, just as the bygone painters once did.

Lenox

IN SUMMERTIME, when the living is easy, this serene town in western Massachusetts becomes a bustling hub of artistic activity. First there is Tanglewood, the idyllic summer home of the Boston Symphony Orchestra, where music is constantly being played or taught—symphonic, chamber, popular, jazz—making the nearby Berkshire hills come alive with the sound of, well, music. At Shakespeare & Company, the play's the thing—eight plays are usually up and running, in fact, on three indoor and outdoor stages. A visitor can picnic on the grounds, stroll the forest trails and catch a free alfresco family performance at Bankside. The Mount Estate and Gardens (above), an elegant 1902 mansion where Edith Wharton lived and wrote, must be visited, as must the Ventfort Hall Museum of the Gilded Age. In towns near Lenox, there is more: the Berkshire Museum in Pittsfield, the Massachusetts Museum of Contemporary Art (Mass MoCA) in North Adams, the Norman Rockwell Museum in Stockbridge, the Jacob's Pillow dance festival in Becket. And every shunpike that you take leads to more summer theater; the Williamstown Theatre Festival lures the stars of Broadway each year, as well as thousands of avid patrons.

Montezuma

WHY IN THE WORLD are we sending our culture vultures to a sun-splashed little village in Costa Rica known principally for its beach (below) and the scenic waterfalls outside of town? Because we want to introduce them to yet another hot trend in vacationing: the language holiday. High school and college kids have long spent parts of their summers at tutorial classes in noncampus settings, but now various tourism companies are pitching programs to any traveler who might want to bring a little learning back from vacation. Most of these programs involve daily foreign-language instruction, and all of them make certain to include recreational opportunities on a daily basis as well. The one in Montezuma, which is run by La Escuela del Sol, offers Spanish lessons in sessions ranging from one to four weeks. Your choice of add-ons includes yoga (90 minutes a day), surfing (two hours of coaching a day) or poi—the art of fire dancing (again, 90 minutes each day). There are also horseback trips to the famous waterfalls and nighttime giant turtle egg–laying tours. You will return from Costa Rica feeling fit, refreshed—and maybe just a little bit smarter.

KEVIN SPRAGUE

CRAIG LOVELL/AURORA

THE FRENCH ARTIST Auguste Rodin, who was born in 1840 and died in 1917, is regarded as the father of modern sculpture; he is perhaps, with Michelangelo, one of the two most famous sculptors who ever lived. Bronzes made from his most masterly casts—*The Thinker, The Kiss, The Gates of Hell, The Burghers of Calais*—are on display in museums dedicated almost wholly to his legacy. If you find yourself in Paris, by all means visit the Musée Rodin, which was opened in 1919 in the Hôtel Biron, where Rodin used to stay. Here at home, if you are in Philadelphia, do take in the Rodin Museum. And we have a recommendation for visitors to

The Rodin
Sculpture
Garden

California: the Rodin Sculpture Garden on the campus of Stanford University in Palo Alto. Stanford's collection of Rodin bronzes, to which this burgher (below) belongs, is the largest in the world outside Paris. The setting that has been found for the 20 works on display outside the Cantor Art Center is sublime; the monumental *Gates of Hell,* which was inspired by Dante and which consumed Rodin for two decades, is here in its awesomeness and can be experienced at any hour, as it is lit for nighttime viewing. Inside are more than 50 of his works, mostly in cast bronze but also in wax, plaster and terra-cotta. The full effect is astounding.

JOEL SIMON IMAGES

CLARO CORTES IV/LANDOV

Nanjing

IN DIFFERENT ERAS, artists, particularly those of an experimental or otherwise unusual sort, have had a hard time of it in China. But in the long—very, very long— history of Nanjing, creative people have almost always found a comfortable home here. Human inhabitancy of the region where Nanjing now exists dates back 300,000 years. One of China's four ancient capitals, Nanjing served as the country's ultimate seat of power in several dynasties. But more significant to our point: The city was the cultural keystone of China for 10 dynasties, and it feeds off and seeks to perpetuate that tradition. There are dance troupes, opera houses, music ensembles and poetry collectives galore. In the visual arts, there is even what might be called an avant-garde. "Nanjing artists are different," Guo Haiping, a 30-something painter and restaurateur, told *Time* magazine. "We're not like those serious, solitary-minded Beijing or Shanghai artists." In the present day, Nanjing's art is allowed to flower in the open, even unto the outdoor Basking in the Sunshine festival of art installations down by the Yangtze River. China is changing, and Nanjing has been anticipating that change.

THE IMPOSSIBLE DREAM ▶

Carnegie Hall

THE OLD JOKE has a tourist asking, "How do I get to Carnegie Hall?" to which the wiseacre New Yorker answers, "Practice, practice, practice." It's good advice, although the truth is you don't have to be a Tchaikovsky or a Mahler or a Bernstein to play the place (even if those three found it helpful). You can rent Carnegie Hall if you've got the considerable lucre and the chutzpah—and, crucially, if there is an open date. One recent example: The glorious 2,804-seat Stern Auditorium (Carnegie's main hall, right) was booked for March 19, 2008, by the . . . University of Iowa Symphony Band, which wanted to do something special to celebrate the retirement of its director, Myron Welch. Iowa's is a fine band, no doubt, but you would expect to find it performing in Iowa City, right? So then: Keep practicing, and when you're ready, give the folks at Carnegie a buzz. The big stage awaits!

The Inside Passage

ALASKA SEEMS A COLD, forbidding place to many. Were they to travel the Inside Passage, the 500-mile-long stretch of the Alaskan panhandle that is home to a thousand islands and 15,000 miles of shoreline, they would not only be pleasantly surprised, they would be fairly amazed. Prevailing here is a mild maritime climate that beckons to kayakers and canoeists, as well as to cruise ships filled with tourists who harbor far different ideas of what constitutes a pleasure craft. The visitors thrill at the wildlife—sea lions, porpoises, whales, bald eagles—and at the active tidewater glaciers and stunning 3,000-foot cliffs that rise straight up from sea channels, such as this one in Glacier Bay. The southern panhandle is dominated by the 16.8-million-acre Tongass rainforest, and elsewhere are picturesque villages reflecting various histories and cultures of the region: Ancient Native American totem poles send a signal in Haines, while a Russian heritage is apparent in Sitka. Skagway and Ketchikan were gold rush boomtowns back when, and they celebrate their legacy with evocative old saloons and horse-drawn carriages. Inside the Inside Passage is an Alaska welcoming to all.

58° 22' N, 134° 34' W

Morocco by Camel

LET'S FACE IT, THERE IS PLAYACTING going on when a modern tourist signs on for a camel trek through Morocco. None of us is Lawrence of Arabia, much less the far more authentic Berber nomads of Saharan history and prehistory. We would look somewhere between out of place and downright silly in those robes. And now for the "But": Camel trekking through Morocco is terrific fun and an available-to-all adventure that affords wonderful opportunities to enjoy fantastic desert scenery and allows the imagination to run. The golden dunes of the western fringes of the Sahara rise as high as 55 yards above the desert floor; as they shimmer before you, they mesmerize. On tours of a single day or up to two weeks, there will certainly be an oasis involved, and on the longer treks there will be visits to modern-day Berber villages and nomadic tribes of sheep herders, people who are as at home in this environment as you are a fish out of water. Isn't this really what tourism is? A step from your world into another's.

32° 0′ N, 5° 0′ W

DALLAS AND JOHN HEATON/CORB

Phuket by Elephant

THIS IS A DIFFERENT BEAST than your Moroccan camel trek. It is not measured in days and starry, starry nights but in hours and even half-hours—it's a short and sweet visit with the elephants. Now, there are many places throughout Thailand where one might interact with domesticated pachyderms, but we choose to highlight Phuket. Why? Because it is an often lovely island, with sandy beaches, dramatic mountains and, in the north, dense rainforest. We also select Phuket to let you know that this place, which was overrun by the devastating 2004 tsunami, is in fine shape. The same cannot be said, sadly, for the Asian elephant. Habitat encroachment, poaching and other causes have reduced the Thai elephant population from 100,000 circa 1900 to about 4,000 today. How does elephant trekking improve their lot, if at all? Well, the most reputable firms (and please do research beforehand, and choose an outfit that's doing right by its animals) are trying to raise money to support all of the nation's elephants with proper food, medicine and care. It's nice when you can do a bit of good while enjoying yourself. What is usually involved in one of these treks is a ride up into the hills, where there are scenic vistas and also, at the right times of day, opportunities to visit with monkeys and gibbons. Beyond the altruism, it is a fun and exciting way to spend an afternoon, particularly for the kids.

The Masai Mara

WE SHOULD PAUSE HERE for a moment to point out the obvious: We live in a troubled world, and a few of the dream destinations in our book are in very troubled places. Kenya, as we know, has had difficulties in recent times, so you'll want to monitor the situation before flying to Nairobi. But if and when you are able to travel to this eastern African nation, make certain not to miss the Masai Mara. The former word refers to the native people of the area, the latter to the region, and taken together they indicate a large reserve that includes the Serengeti Plains of southwestern Kenya and northern Tanzania, home to a bountiful population of wildlife of all stripes (ask the zebras). The "Big Five"—buffalo, elephant, leopard, lion and rhinoceros—are here, as are the cheetah, giraffe, hippo, jackal, mongoose, warthog and more than a dozen kinds of antelope, from bushbuck and dik-dik to waterbuck and wildebeest (seen here). Among primates we have the galago, baboon and monkey. There are lodges and camps to house you, and guides to lead your safari. The rolling grasslands provide an unsurpassed backdrop for spotting the animals, which proceed at a natural pace through their own often violent existences, largely oblivious to the human tribulations around them.

0°1'S, 0°36'E

The Burren

THE SCENIC SPLENDORS of Ireland are many, from the rolling beauty of the Ring of Kerry in the southwest to the mammoth stepping stones into the sea called the Giant's Causeway in the far north. Despite the recent economic boom in the Republic, there remain quaint villages and narrow one-lane roads bordered by hedgerows where crossing cows and sheep will bring traffic to a halt. Perhaps best reflecting the mystical but rough-hewn side of the Irish personality is the Burren in County Clare. To hike this moonscape of rocky land, where hills and vales are marked by ruined castles that once belonged to local chieftains, is an eerie but moving experience. Ireland's prehistory is here, represented by ring forts and (opposite) megalithic portal tombs: boulder-lined hollows built into the landscape by ancient pagans who sent their dead to the afterlife from these "passage graves." The rugged Aran Islands just offshore are kin to the Burren, and if you think of the tight knit and intricate patterns in a coarse-wool Aran Island sweater—these days a fashion item far beyond the islands—you get a sense of this place where the wind whistles off the sea and ghosts are in the air.

RICHARD T. NOWITZ/CORBIS

The Bosporus

LINKING EUROPE WITH ASIA by water and running right through the heart of Turkish Istanbul, the Bosporus Strait connects the Sea of Mamara with the Black Sea. Every day the strait teems with watercraft, from large ships to small fishing boats to all manner of conveyance for the tourist. A boat tour will, indeed, be your best introduction. As you cruise the Bosporus's 20-mile length, you gaze up at a shoreline that rises dramatically to 650 feet in places. Atop the cliffs are palaces, fortresses, ruins, grand houses, mosques (above, Istanbul's Suleymaniye Mosque), villages, gardens—any of them worthy of exploration. This ancient city of Istanbul, the only one in the world to straddle two continents, has gone by different names—Byzantium, Constantinople—and has played various roles, usually as a capital city and principal port for, sequentially, the Greeks, Romans, Persians, Arabs and Ottoman Turks. Today, Istanbul and the magnificent strait that traverses it conspire to create exotic, priceless memories for all who travel there.

0° 03'N, 114° 0'E

Borneo's Rainforests

IN THE SOUTH CHINA SEA and Pacific Ocean off Southeast Asia lie many islands, including the world's third largest, Borneo. This is a geographically spectacular realm, with mountains as high as two miles above sea level, mighty rivers more than 500 miles long, caves that are as large as any in the world. Ecologically, Borneo is similarly endowed: 15,000 species of flowering plants, 3,000 kinds of trees, more than 200 species of mammals and 420 of birds. Home to many of these plants and animals has always been the highland rainforests. The endangered Bornean orangutan lives here, as do the similarly beleaguered Asian elephant, Sumatran rhinoceros and Bornean clouded leopard. The good news is that the forests, though much depleted by logging and other habitat pressures, are still with us. The bad news is that they and some of their most famous denizens are under constant threat. The Malaysian plywood industry continues to devour trees at a voracious pace, and burgeoning palm oil plantations are equally hungry for acreage. Go to Borneo. See this land of unequalled biodiversity while you still can. Once you've been, if you feel inspired and are so inclined, do your bit to protect this amazing place.

Great St. Bernard Pass

NAPOLEON TRAVELED BY THIS ROUTE, and so did, earlier, the mighty Huns. Even earlier, Julius Caesar used the pass, and circa 300 B.C., Bronze Age hunter-gatherers left evidence of their presence here. This way through the mountains, which connects Switzerland with Italy at an altitude of 8,100 feet, is the oldest path across the western Alps. It was named for Bernard of Menthon, who would minister to travelers undone by the pass in the 11th century. Bernard, who oversaw the building of a hospice here, was beatified shortly after his death and he was later declared patron saint of the Alps. Those are considerable honors, to be sure, but another fine posthumous accolade came his way when a strange hybrid dog, a large, slobbering cross between a mastiff and a Great Dane or perhaps a Newfoundland, was named the St. Bernard. The dogs have a noble history at the pass, where they served on rescue missions for three centuries (though the restorative brandy cask on their collars is an Alpine legend). Monks at the hospice (opposite) welcome thousands of tourists in summer and a few intrepid high-country skiers in winter, when the road is closed. And they still care for the dogs.

Bucks County

LET US SAY THAT IT IS AUTUMN. The leaves in the Northeast are ablaze, reds and oranges and yellows commingling in a riotous symphony of outrageously brilliant hues. Every year at this time, you get behind the wheel and head for the hills. You revel in the gracious countryside, the small town centers, the occasional antique store, the many pumpkin stands, the covered bridges. So where are you, other than in paradise? Vermont, surely, or maybe New Hampshire? Maine or Massachusetts? You must be somewhere in New England, foliage capital of the world? No, you are on a road (somewhat) less traveled but no less resplendent. Bucks County, Pennsylvania, could compete with any upcountry hamlet in a Currier & Ives contest. We're not talking about Lower Bucks here, which is a thickly settled part of suburban Philadelphia. We're referring instead to the rural parts farther north. To drive Route 32, more poetically known as River Road, from Washington Crossing to New Hope on a glorious fall day is to come to an inescapable conclusion: New England's got nothing on this.

CARL CHRISTENSEN/INTEGRITY STUDIO

The Orient Express

IT CAN GET A BIT CONFUSING, what with the Orient Express name and cachet having been loaned to (or co-opted by) various rail and even cruise lines, and with the original Orient Express, which made its maiden run from Paris to Giurgiu, Romania, on October 4, 1883, having had its route greatly shortened over the years. First, some history: By the 1930s, the line's reputation was at its zenith, with three luxury services crossing Europe by different routes. (Trivia: Agatha Christie's 1934 mystery classic, *Murder on the Orient Express,* is not set on the original line but on the Simplon Orient Express, which connected Paris with Istanbul on a southerly route through Milan and Venice.) In recent years,

high-speed trains have chipped away at the edges of the legendary line, but there are still a couple of ways to replicate—and thoroughly enjoy—the Orient Express experience. First, you can book a sleeper car on what's left of the original route—a train runs nightly between two of Europe's loveliest cities, Strasbourg and Vienna. Or you can take a trip on a privately owned line bearing the Orient Express name; more than one of these rolls regularly across Europe and even China (below, chugging through Germany's Black Forest). The vintage trains employ restored coaches from the 1920s and '30s in their largely successful effort to recall a bygone age and to recreate a timeless sense of style.

Le Marche

EVER SINCE THE DISCOVERY of Italy's sublime Tuscan region more than a decade ago, there have been many nominees for "the new Tuscany." It's a silly game. No more than Tuscany was "the new Provence" (and it certainly was dubbed that at one point) are these other places stand-ins for the original. Having said that, if you want pastoral Italy without the fleets of tour buses to be found in the more on-the-beaten-path destinations, you must try Le Marche (pronounced "lay markay"). All but hidden in the east-central part of the country, this province is marked by rolling hills covered with shimmering gray-green olive groves and vineyards. There are charming villages with shops, markets and small grace notes (here, a violin-maker in Ascoli Piceno). There are countryside accents: ancient churches and ruined castles that seem to have been placed just so in the landscape by a master planner with a Martha Stewart touch. The Esino and Potenza rivers flow through Le Marche, and in their valleys are working farms, some of which offer room and board. Le Marche receives about a tenth as many visits from foreigners as Tuscany does in any given year, and as Martha would aver: That's a good thing.

The Huangshan Mountains

IN CHINESE ART there are often depicted strange, almost surreal mountains of unnatural steepness and grandeur, enshrouded in swirling mists in their higher realms. Believe it or not, this is representational art; these mountains exist and are as dramatic as anything our imaginations might conjure. The Huangshan range in eastern China was once buried beneath an ancient sea, and later carved by glaciers. The ice did magnificent work, leaving behind dozens of the world's most impressive peaks and notches, including Huangshan's Grand Canyon (seen here). The tallest mountains—Bright Summit

Peak, Celestial Peak and Lotus Flower Peak—have summits more than 6,000 feet above sea level, and many others exceed 3,000 feet. The entire, largely forested range, which was declared a UNESCO World Heritage Site in 1990, has an ethereal beauty. There are hot springs at the base of Purple Cloud Peak, and due to climactic conditions in the area, mists often form below the tops of the mountains, creating a fabulous visual effect on high known as "the sea of clouds." The Huangshans are a destination of choice for the Chinese, and for anyone who revels in extraordinary Alpine landscape.

30° 0′ N, 118° 0′ E •

Lake Okeechobee

27° 0′ N, 80° 53′ W •

ACCORDING TO ESTIMATES, there are nearly 50 million bird-watchers in the United States, an enormous army of keen observers of our fine avian friends. Every one of these birders should put Florida's Lake Okeechobee on his or her life list of places to visit. Okeechobee, known to locals as the Big Lake, is in fact the second-largest body of freshwater in the Lower 48, after Lake Michigan. Situated as it is, equidistant between the Atlantic and the Gulf of Mexico in southern Florida, it attracts both marine and inland birds. Though large (730 square miles), it is shallow (an average depth of nine feet and a maximum of 12), and therefore wading birds such as egrets, wood ibis, sandhill cránes and blue herons are right at home here. Seen above are woodstorks gathering in a rookery in spring to raise their young. Bald eagles, pileated woodpeckers, ospreys and red-shouldered hawks nest nearby, and the rare Everglades kite can be found in the southwest section of the lake, feeding on apple snails. Cardinals are plentiful, and during migrations there are warblers; painted buntings and indigo buntings are also drop-in visitors. For birders, the trail around the lake is a pathway to enchantment.

Eden

WHO KNEW? WHO WOULD ever have guessed that in the new millennium, Eden would be found not somewhere in the Middle East but far from the Holy Land in a clay pit located outside a village in a depressed, rugged, regularly rainy corner of England? The corner would be the southwestern one, in the county of Cornwall. The man behind the Eden Project is Tim Smit, a music producer with a background in archaeology, whose overarching passion is for ecological awareness. He imagined a world-beating environmental science center for Bodelva, Cornwall, dominated by two fantastic "biomes" (giant greenhouses, the world's largest). And by golly, he raised more than $100 million and got the thing done, even though the final building season in 2000 and 2001 featured—get this—134 straight days of rain. Then Eden, against further odds, became a roaring success: It's more popular as a tourist attraction than the Tower of London, and has already enticed nearly 10 million Brits and foreigners to visit Bodelva and its amazing indoor rainforest. There is much more to Eden than what's growing inside the greenhouses—interactive learning exhibits as well as groves of native plants outside, for example — all of it geared to raising environmental consciousness. Smit has said that he wanted to build the Eighth Wonder of the World, but what he really wants to do is save the planet.

44° 38' N, 63° 35' W

Nova Scotia

AT ONE POINT in the famous Carly Simon song, the vain one flies his "Lear jet up to Nova Scotia/To see the total eclipse of the sun." This coastal province in southeastern Canada is indeed a perfect place for such an astronomical experience, what with the air being so crisp and clear, particularly in the northern part of the peninsula up by the Gulf of St. Lawrence. (In the south near the Atlantic, it can often get foggy.) A visit to Nova Scotia provides a variety of pleasures: the maritime scenery of a coastal drive, the pastoral beauty of the rural precincts inland, the rich cultural offerings in the province's capital, Halifax. And right outside of the city, it is serenely arcadian in places; the scene below is of Peggy's Cove in St. Margaret's Bay. In Nova Scotia, you will correctly infer native Mi'kmaq, French, African and Celtic influences at play in the cuisine, the art, the music—and, indeed, in the people around you. Make sure to drive across the Strait of Canso to Cape Breton Island. Named by *Condé Nast Traveler* magazine the most beautiful island anywhere, it is also one of the world's hotbeds of Celtic music. Go there. Relax in a pub. The fire is warm, and so is the fiddle.

CHAD EHLERS/AURORA

GERALD BRIMACOMBE

59° 17' N, 18° 3' E

Stockholm and Its Islands

SWEDEN'S SENSATIONAL capital city is, as we see above, built on islands—14 of them. We speak here of these islands and of 24,000 others (yes, you read that right) that dot the Baltic Sea in an area around Stockholm approximately 40 miles long. In summertime, the wondrous Stockholm archipelago, bathed in sunshine for 18 hours a day, is as radiant as any place on earth. The larger islands have harbors and towns—the year-round population on the archipelago is 10,000—while thousands of the smallest are uninhabited. There are some 50,000 vacation cottages sprinkled about, many of them privately owned and used by locals, but lots of others are available to tourists. Whether for a day trip or longer (there are good choices of hotels, hostels and bed-and-breakfasts), take a steamship out to the islands. Enjoy seafood in the open air on the cluster of islands called Fjäderholmarna. Tour the archipelago museum, which is housed in a 16th-century fort on Vaxholm. Take a peaceful walk on Finnhamm or Möja, just a bit farther out. This is island hopping of the very highest order.

53° 4′ N, 4° 5′ W

Snowdonia

SERIOUS MOUNTAIN CLIMBERS come to this region and its eponymous national park hard by the Irish Sea in North Wales, but you do not need to be the least bit athletic to avail yourself of the quirky pleasures of Snowdonia. You can, for instance, take the Snowdon Mountain Railway to the summit of the park's signature peak. Or you can simply gaze at the beautiful mountain range from the porch of your bed-and-breakfast in the charming village of Betws-y-Coed (population about 600), which nestles at the confluence of the Conwy and Llugwy rivers inside the park. Take a walk to the scenic vantage point overlooking the twin lakes of Llynnau Mymbyr (seen here) or visit the local, preciously named sheepdog center, Ewe-Phoria, and see these diligent canines at work. Wander around Dolwyddelan and Gwydir castles, pondering as you do the legends, many involving dragons or a monster and one starring Merlin himself, associated with this place. Two botanical treats not to be missed: Bodnant Gardens and the Conwy Valley Garden Maze. At more than two acres in size, this construct of English yew is one of the world's largest hedge mazes, and one more wonderful way to lose yourself in Snowdonia.

Reykjavik

THE PLANET'S NORTHERNMOST capital city is one hot town, literally and figuratively. It is hot in its famous geothermal pools that represent nirvana to bathers. (Opposite: the Blue Lagoon spa outside town. There is, as the picture implies, so much volcanic activity going on beneath Iceland that Reykjavik is able to keep most of the city's houses warm via the world's largest geothermal heating system.) And Reykjavik is hot in another way, too: as a nightlife hub. Young people and old from throughout the country and beyond descend on Reykjavik's 100-plus bars and clubs every weekend, and party till quitting time, which is usually at about 6 a.m. Furthermore, as Iceland is a small country, all manner of scenic splendor is within easy reach of the city. Right nearby are geysers, lava formations and thunderous waterfalls. In the Westfjords, there are picturesque fishing villages and, right behind them, imposing mountains. Its proximity to the Arctic Circle means Reykjavik can count on performances by the northern lights in the winter sky. Iceland's only city: the world's unlikeliest hot spot.

CATHERINE KARNOW/AURORA

Transylvania

THERE'S NOTHING NIGHTMARISH about this large and legendary province in the middle of Romania, though it's true that in the distant past a lot of blood was spilled here in unspeakable ways. Transylvania is an inspiring land of breathtaking mountains, lovely villages, impressive castles and even, in the culturally hopping town of Sibiu, cafe society. Brasov and Sighisoara are two of the finest examples of medieval cities left in the world. The latter has a walled citadel perched on a hilltop, secret gateways to back alleys, a 14th-century clock tower and, oh yes, a house where Prince Vlad Tepes was supposedly born in the mid-1400s. Outside Brasov is the intimidating Bran Castle (above) where Vlad reigned, rather forcefully, as Prince of Wallachia. His pro-wrestling–style nickname, you might know, was "The Impaler"—and it was a well-earned moniker. When the 19th-century Irish novelist Bram Stoker created his memorable vampire, Dracula, he may or may not have had Vlad in mind, but he certainly set the action in Vlad's neighborhood. The bloodsucker's fame might seem to be an everlasting curse for the Transylvania tourist board, but the urging here is: Break the spell.

Under the Sea

THAT GREAT DREAMER Jules Verne would have loved it: submarine excursions for the whole family. Various operations around the world are in this game—there's Submarines Australasia in New Zealand's Milford Sound and Hurghada Sinbad Submarines, which will take you beneath the Red Sea —but the firm that dominates and that is represented in these pictures, is Atlantis Submarine Tours. The company has a fleet of 11 custom-designed subs operating throughout the Caribbean, in Guam and in the Hawaiian islands of Oahu, Kona and Maui— each cost more than $3 million to build. Some carry 48 passengers, others 64, and for about $100 a trip, you can make like Nemo and explore the depths.

COURTESY ATLANTIS ADVENTURES (2)

Banff and Lake Louise

WINTER OR SUMMER, the Canadian Rockies represent a sensational venue for recreation, and the picture-perfect western town of Banff, in Alberta, is the hub of all activity. In summer, the hiking and mountain climbing are unparalleled, and to engage in milder pursuits such as golf, tennis and lounging in the valleys below, surrounded by fir forests and jagged peaks, is vacationing at its best. In winter, Banff and its environs are, if anything, even more stimulating. The skiing is world-class—in fact, the World Cup circuit visits the area for races each season—and heli-skiing is plentiful for the truly intrepid. If you have the wherewithal, by all means stay at either the legendary Banff Springs Hotel or the equally grand Chateau Lake Louise (seen here), which is up the mountain road a piece. The perfect day: You rise as the sun comes over the mountains, enjoy a sumptuous repast and are the first skier to track the new powder that has fallen in the back bowls of the Lake Louise ski area. You schuss hard for a few hours, then head back to the Chateau for a late lunch and perhaps a nap. Before dinner, you take a solitary ski on the cross-country trails or perhaps a turn on the hotel's ice-skating rink. After dinner, you and yours enjoy a spin around the frozen lake in a horse-drawn sleigh. Then a nightcap of brandy or a cup of cocoa, and off to bed. The following day: Repeat.

51° 10′ N, 115° 34′ W

Golf in Oregon

HERE'S THE THING ABOUT A GOLF VACATION: You have to be able to get on the course. Many of the country's finest layouts are vigorously private, and if you do not have an invitation from a member, then your situation is futile. There's no point in vacationing near Pine Valley or Augusta National in hopes that your hangdog expression will win you access to the first tee. So, what to do? Many of the greatest courses in other countries, even those attached to private clubs, will allow visitors to play for a princely sum, and you can indeed book a tour of the most famous links of Scotland or Ireland. In America, you can line up to play at Pebble Beach or Pinehurst Number 2 or the Black Course at Bethpage State Park, each of which has hosted the U.S. Open and each of which allows you to buy your way on. Then there are areas with clusters of fine, daily-fee courses; Myrtle Beach in South Carolina comes quickly to mind. We choose to highlight Oregon, a phenomenon in the modern American golfing experience. In recent years, golf course architects have realized that the scenery and lay of the land near the Oregon coast and inland are just about perfect for an ideal experience of the game. And we now have such splendid options as Pacific Dunes, Bandon Trails and Bandon Dunes (seen here)— and that's in Bandon alone! Playing Crosswater, Pumpkin Ridge or the Running Y Ranch is just as challenging, and just as much fun. The golf in Oregon isn't free, but it is fine.

The Sun Kosi River

28° 0' N, 83° 0' E

LET'S SAY YOU DREAM of Himalayan adventure but aren't up for a shot at Everest. Trust us: You have options. One of the finest is a white-water rafting excursion on Nepal's "River of Gold." The Sun Kosi rises near Tibet's Mount Shisha Pangma and runs east through the Mahabharat Lekh range and the Himalayas, the world's highest mountains. As it approaches India's northern plains, where it will join the Ganges and proceed to the Bay of Bengal, it becomes the river equivalent of the Himalayas: mighty, beautiful, sometimes fierce. An expedition on the Sun Kosi, which can last more than a week and cover more than 150 miles, most of it in pure wilderness, will feature rapids from Class 2 to Class 5. You will shake, rattle and roll through stretches that have earned such nicknames as High Anxiety, Jaws and the Big Dipper. Around and above you will be those tremendous mountains: an unrivaled backdrop for what is guaranteed to be a thrilling once-in-a-lifetime experience.

ANDERS BLOMQUIST/GETTY

Kiawah Island

ONE OF THE MOST CAREFULLY PRESERVED barrier islands in the world, South Carolina's Kiawah has 10,000 acres of maritime forests, tidal marshes and lagoons. It is home to shorebirds and fish, and, as might be imagined, is a walker's or cyclist's or canoeist's dream. The 10-mile long island is developed in places, with a gated community, resort lodgings, a general store (The Market at Town Center); and at the crossroads of John, Kiawah and Seabrook islands is Freshfields Village, where you will find stores as well as restaurants. Golfers are as happy as clams on Kiawah, but, we want to note, the tennis is just as fine. In fact, the tennis at the Kiawah Island Golf Resort, which has 28 courts, is ranked among the very best in the country. For a vacationer who likes vigorous activity every morning followed by a little communing with nature after lunch, Kiawah Island is a destination of choice.

COURTESY KIAWAH ISLAND GOLF AND TENNIS RESORT

Denali

NEEDLESS TO SAY, there are winter recreations to be enjoyed
in Alaska. Yes, it's cold in the 49th state, and certainly this vast
land experiences more than its fair share of darkness. But there
are fine ski areas and, for the heartiest among us, winter hiking
and mountain-climbing opportunities. In the national park
and reserve surrounding the great Denali—that storied peak,
America's very tallest, which is also known as Mount McKinley—
there is dog sledding. Various firms and lodges offer training
and trips for neophyte and experienced mushers both. There
are journeys that overnight in backcountry cabins and others
that feature heated tents; there are valley trips and high-country
trips. Traveling in the Denali wilderness in winter, a visitor is
guaranteed clear views of the Alaska Range and starry nights
regularly featuring an appearance of the spectacular aurora
borealis, also known as the northern lights. There will also be
wildlife sightings that may include moose, caribou, fox, wolverine
and Dall sheep. At bedtime, the howls of dogs tethered outside
will mingle with the haunting cry of a wolf.

Provence

43° 32′ N, 5° 25′ E

THE TOUR DE FRANCE is the world's most famous cycling competition for a variety of reasons, including the French passion for the sport and the challenge posed to the competitors by the jagged reaches of the Alps. Not to be overlooked when assessing the allure of the Tour, however, is this: There are precious few more attractive places to cycle in the world than the French countryside. The Provence region can be enjoyed in any conveyance, but it is best experienced by bicycle. Book yourself a guided or self-guided week-long excursion in late spring, and pedal from village to village, enjoying scenery that changes along the way, always trumping itself. Fields of fruit trees, lavender and olive groves yield, just around a corner, to an astonishing spray of poppies, then a glimpse of the Rhône River shimmering blindingly in the sun, and then—over there!—the landmark windwill Moulin Daudet. Coast down in to the next charming town—Fontaine-de-Vaucluse or Isle-sur-la-Sorgue or Oppède-le-Vieux or Menerbes or Lacoste or Bonnieux or Nîmes or Fontvieille—on narrow roads called *chemins,* and stop briefly to assemble your picnic at the market. Fresh bread, certainly, and cheese, olives, pears and, perhaps, a bottle of *vin ordinaire.* Spread your blanket wherever you choose on the gray-green grass. It's all good.

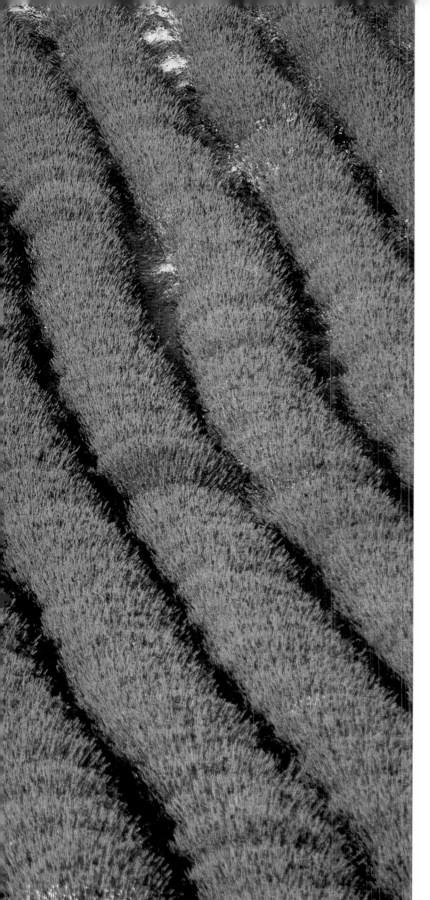

Anahola Bay

BREAKING NEWS: The surfing in Hawaii's pretty darn good! Okay, okay: You've already heard. You've heard about Waikiki and the legend of Duke Kahanamoku and the monster waves of the North Shore and the whole there's-nothing-like-surfing-in-Hawaii mishegas. Is there any such a thing, you wonder, as a secret Hawaii for surfers? A beach not yet discovered; the surfing version of the private fishing hole? No, there really isn't—but there are sands that are relatively less disturbed than others and breaks that are less crowded. If you haven't visited Anahola Bay, boogie board or surfboard in tow, you should. First, your trip gets you to the island of Kauai, arguably the most spectacular, mile for mile, of any of the six Hawaiian islands that are frequented by tourists. Do spend time investigating this paradise, a veritable Bali Hai, then head to Anahola Bay in the northeast corner of the island. There you will find a protected cove: a curve of sand with part of the tide interrupted by coral reefs and bordered at one end by Kuaehu Point and at the other by Kahala Point. The sea here is calm and this is a family beach—no surfing allowed. But right around the bend is the cowabunga section of the bay and the waves are terrific, dude.

22° 15′ N, 159° 31′ W

The Netherlands

THIS IS A LAND OF WATER. There is water, water everywhere, and the Dutch countryside is laced with canals: arteries connecting town with town, here with there. The Netherlands is also, in winter, a land of cold, very often a frigid cold. The canals freeze over, and when they do the citizens lace up their skates. Toddlers do this and grand-parents do also; to be Dutch and not to skate is to be a fish that does not swim. These people celebrate their skating passion on a daily basis (as here, in Kinderdijk)—many kids still skate to school and adults skate to work—but they exalt this passion in the coldest years by staging the Elfstedentocht (Eleven Towns Tour) in the northern province of Friesland. The way to think of this competition: It is the Boston Marathon of skating, as much a cultural event as a contest. About 300 competitive skaters are truly racing against each other, while the balance of the 16,000 entrants are engaged in a leisure excursion. The start of the 125-mile event is in the pre-dawn darkness of Leeuwarden, the cap-ital of Friesland, and a skater must complete the circuit and return to the city by midnight. Some 600,000 citizens of the province pour forth throughout the day to cheer the competitors on. If you are a serious skater, you should look into the Elfstedentocht—but be informed, it doesn't go off every year, only when the entire route is frozen solid.

39° 10' S, 175° 38' E

The Tongariro
Northern Circuit

NEW ZEALAND SPORTS some of the world's very best hiking—or tramping—routes, called "tracks" and collectively known as the New Zealand Great Walks. Rigorously maintained with well-kept huts and other amenities, these nine backcountry hikes set an international standard and lure thousands of visitors to the "other" land down under each year. There is variety here: The high-Alpine experience of the Kepler Track is in stark contrast to the beach walks along the Abel Tasman Coast Track and to the even more watery experience of the Whanganui Journey, which isn't really a hike at all but rather a kayak excursion on the country's longest navigable river. The temptation is always to highlight the Milford Track, one of the most famous mountain-going adventures in the world this side of climbing Everest. While several days on the Milford certainly make for a memorable experience, the track is so popular in the New Zealand summer that traffic on it is always heavy and also regulated. Less well-traveled but no less spectacular is the Tongariro Northern Circuit, a loop around a symmetrical volcano, Mount Ngauruhoe, that rises in the middle of New Zealand's North Island. The trek usually takes three nights in the backcountry, and if you go, here's a tip: Since you are already traveling such a long way, start saving your pennies now for a night's accommodation on either end of your walk at the nearby Grand Chateau—a delightfully luxurious add-on to one of the best possible hiking vacations.

FREDERICK CHARLES

PER-ANDRE HOFFMANN/GETTY

Cooperstown

THIS IS A VILLAGE OF some 2,000 citizens in central New York state where baseball was decidedly *not* invented by Abner Doubleday in a cow pasture in 1839. No, baseball was not born here—it evolved earlier, largely down in New York City and in Hoboken, New Jersey—and neither was James Fenimore Cooper. He, too, came from Jersey, at age one, when his family relocated to a site at the south end of Otsego Lake. The village is actually named after the author's father, William, who is considered Cooperstown's founder. The son is honored in town with the Fenimore Art Museum, which boasts a strong Hudson River School collection as well as artifacts pertaining to Cooper and his family. Cooperstown is also home to the esteemed Glimmerglass Opera, the Farmers' Museum and great fishing and boating. Folks here are always insisting that there's much more to the town than baseball. That's true, but since 1939 the reason fans trek to Cooperstown, like they do to Fenway Park or Wrigley Field, is to bask in the glow of our national pastime at the hallowed National Baseball Hall of Fame and Museum. For problematical reasons, Barry Bonds and Roger Clemens may never get in—but you can.

Lillehammer

OLD OLYMPIC TOWNS ARE LEFT with legacies: maybe a monetary profit or a bill still due, certainly a heightened profile on the world stage, and always a lot of bequeathed infrastructure. There are new stadiums to be maintained, arcane playing fields to be dealt with. *What shall we do with that archery venue?* Particularly for the host towns and cities of the Winter Games, the left-behind Olympic site is a true boon. Skating rinks and ski areas have been brought up to world-class standards, and exotica like luge and bobsled runs are also now available as tourist attractions. Lillehammer was a lovely town in Norway with a reputation for winter recreation opportunities long before the Olympics arrived in 1994. Now it is a place to be visited by any cold-weather sportsperson at least once in a lifetime. The Hafjell downhill resort is barely 10 miles from the city, and a system of more than 200 miles of cross-country trails streams out from downtown into the surrounding forest (right), eventually joining up with the very tracks used during the Games.

Palau

IN THE PACIFIC OCEAN 500 miles east of the Philippines and 2,000 miles south of Japan lies a tropical nation comprising a dozen small island groups—taken as a whole, still one of the tiniest independent countries in the world—that leads all others in an important category: In 1989, an international marine conservation organization called CEDAM ranked Palau first among seven Underwater Wonders of the World. It was also anointed by the famous American television series when in 2005 *Survivor: Palau* drew huge audiences. (The TV folks thought so well of Palau, it was asked to serve as a setting a second time in 2008.) As the CEDAM citation implied and as the televised programs confirmed for any who saw them, this is home to some of the world's very best snorkeling and scuba diving. Off the mellifluously named Floating Garden Islands to the west of Palau's principal island, Koror, or off the Rock Islands just to the south of Koror, exists a marine universe of mesmerizing vitality and otherworldly light. The roads on the islands are mostly dirt and the upper speed limits are about 25 miles per hour, but experiencing Palau isn't about being on the land and driving around. It's about getting there, getting acclimated and going under.

Daytona Beach

EVERY FEBRUARY, this sun-splashed burg on Florida's east coast revs up when NASCAR comes to town for the kickoff (and premier) event of its latest rip-roaring season. Stock car racing on a beach track at Daytona dates back more than a half century, and it has never been bigger than in the present day. Daytona International Speedway can pack in 185,000 spectators who thrill as the Dales and Tonys and Jimmies and Jeffs of NASCAR's upper echelons duel at speeds in excess of 180 miles per hour. Race week in Daytona is another example of a transcendent sporting event—one that has cultural significance extending beyond the contest. It is where NASCAR Nation comes together to reunite, reminisce—and, of course, party. All of the former greats, from King Richard Petty to the legendary Junior Johnson to the Allison boys, are in town, happily engaging with their fans in that special NASCAR way. And by the by: The seashore at Daytona Beach is beautiful and offers a relaxing break from the engines' roar.

Fort William

WHY ARE WE SENDING our outdoorsy types to Scotland? Well, it's not, in this instance, for the golf. And it's not to go monster hunting in Loch Ness. We're sending you to the West Highlands region north of Glasgow to participate in a variety of rough-and-tumble sports, especially mountain biking, which is splendid here. Fort William and the nearby, smaller villages have become, for the knobby-tire set, a destination of longing similar to Yosemite for rock climbers. Unnamed hill and forest trails have been cut all through the area. In the Nevis Range there is the Witch's Trails network, which has played host to a World Cup event every year since 2002 and was also the site of the 2007 mountain-biking World Championships. It is not for the faint-hearted or inexperienced, being rocky, gnarly and steep at regular intervals. The World Cup downhill track on Aonach Mor, with its frightful drop-offs and jumps, is one of the longest and toughest in the world. There are other delights to the Fort William region, not least the scenery. The dominant peak in the area is Ben Nevis (below, its denizens), which at 4,409 feet is the highest mountain in the United Kingdom. Each September, up to 500 elite hill runners take part in the grueling Ben Nevis Race up and down the slopes. The big summer event in town, besides the mountain-biking competition, is the Lochabar Highland Games: contests of strength and speed that have their origins in the pursuits of the ancient clans of Scotland. Fort William is a big, strong place, attracting big, strong athletes.

The Snake River

THE SPRING MELT in the great mountains of Wyoming seems to last forever; for weeks that reach through June and even into July, the mighty, frothy Snake River is a chocolate brown color. Then it starts to clear and fishing season is finally at hand. Anglers head for the upper reaches near the headwaters in Yellowstone National Park, or for put-ins along the 27-mile stretch that meanders through Grand Teton National Park. Drift boats vie in places with rafts and kayaks and, yes, the Snake can get crowded, but that is because it presents one of the world's very finest freshwater fishing experiences. (As if confirmation were needed, the Snake has served as host river for the World Fly-fishing Championship, a rare honor.) Novices can spin-cast for their quarry if they choose, but the Snake was created by nature to exalt the dry-fly experience: fishing as art form. Experts deftly cast their lines, coaxing brown and rainbow trout from the depths of the river. The native fine-spotted Snake River cutthroat trout is not nearly as wary as his relations, and several of these beauties, up to 17 inches and more, may be landed on a good day. Then again, any day angling on the Snake is going to be a good-to-great one.

44° 13'N, 110° 7' W

MICHAEL MELFORD

Key West and
The Marquesas Keys

OUR COUNTRY DOES NOT, in fact, end at Key West, the terminus of the famous Florida Keys that unspool to the southwest from the mainland tip of the state. Thirty miles yet farther west, right about where the Atlantic Ocean meets the Gulf of Mexico, you come across another island group. These small barrier islands circling a central lagoon are the uninhabited (by law) Marquesas Keys. As with Key West, there is all sorts of pirate lore associated with the Marquesas; the wreck of a 17th-century Spanish treasure-hunting galleon lies in 30 feet of water just off the western shores. And as with Key West, there is beyond-belief salt-water game fishing available. While Key West is duly legendary—what with sailfish, blackfin and yellowfin tuna, wahoo, blue marlin, African pompano and all sorts of grouper ready to bite—the Marquesas offer one-stop shopping for a once-in-a-sporting-lifetime opportunity. Here, an ocean-going angler can try for all three elements of the so-called Keys Grand Slam: bonefish, tarpon and permit. Fly fishing for these fantastic fish in this incomparable setting is a rare and rarified experience.

CHAD EHLERS/AURORA

Victoria Falls

AND WHY WOULD the sporty type travel to famous Victoria Falls, by some measures the world's largest waterfall, on the border between Zimbabwe and Zambia in Africa? Why, to bungee jump, of course. You, too, can leap into the void from the falls' bridge and plummet some 360 feet towards the Zambezi River—that's more than twice the height of Niagara. It will only cost you about a hundred dollars and, maybe, a few gray hairs. But it'll also make for unbeatable water cooler conversation come Monday morning:

"What'd ya do over the weekend?"

"Oh, bungee jumped Victoria Falls. You?"

The Forbidden City

SMACK DAB IN THE MIDDLE of Beijing is a collection of nearly a thousand buildings that are some 600 years old, the largest surviving palace complex and largest assemblage of ancient wooden edifices in the world. This is China's ominously named Forbidden City, the imperial palace and court during the Ming and Qing dynasties. Construction of the city, which is set in a rectangle 180 acres in size, began in 1406 and (as can be accomplished in a dynasty) was completed in a remarkably short time, 14 years. A million workers, including 100,000 artisans, were forced into hard labor in Beijing; forests in faraway provinces were mined for their timber, and tremendous stones quarried outside the city were slid into place over the winter ice. Through the centuries, the Forbidden City was attacked, looted and ransacked several times, but it served as an imperial palace right up until 1912 when Puyi, the last emperor of China, abdicated. The city today, well preserved and housing a fascinating history museum, is a glorious if haunting place.

39° 55′ N, 116° 25′ E

Mount Vernon

GEORGE WASHINGTON SLEPT HERE—many times. This stately mansion above the shores of the Potomac River near Alexandria, Virginia, was where our principal Founding Father lived for most of his life. He inherited the estate in 1761 and spent the rest of his days (when he wasn't acting as a military commander or President) expanding it, improving it and managing its five farms. This is the countryside where Washington, who cut an impressive figure and was one of the best horsemen in the land, once rode. These are the fields where tobacco, wheat and other crops once grew, fueling the successful plantation. These are the rooms where George and his wife, Martha, walked and talked (below, the master bedroom). Mount Vernon and its surrounding 500 preserved acres (he actually increased the acreage to 8,000 during his lifetime) are presently in great shape. The mansion, which has been toured by 80 million people since it was first opened to the public in 1860, has recently undergone an expensive and detailed upgrade and is now a state-of-the-art learning center. It has new dioramas, films and interactive displays. But do not worry: You can still see the famous dentures.

MICHAEL MELFORD

JOE RAEDLE/GETTY

The Lewis and Clark National Historic Trail

THE IDEA WAS THOMAS JEFFERSON'S. As early as 1783, when the infant United States had only just emerged from its war of independence with Great Britain, Jefferson approached George Rogers Clark, a hero of that war, and asked him to lead an expedition to explore the continent west of the Mississippi. Clark declined the commission, and Jefferson's hope went unfulfilled for two decades. By 1804, he was the country's third President, and the U.S. had made the Louisiana Purchase and therefore owned immense tracts in the unexplored region. This time, Jefferson's appeal went to Clark's younger brother, William, and to Meriwether Lewis. In May of that year, the two men and their Corps of Discovery set out from the midwestern plains for the Pacific Ocean. They traveled over mountains, along rivers (including the Flathead in Montana, above), on plains and in high-country deserts—and they succeeded. Today, you can retrace their route, learning as you go, through 11 states from Missouri to Washington. Lewis and Clark's journey is one of the seminal American adventure stories, and in regions of the West that are still largely undeveloped and unspoiled, the adventure comes alive.

17° 5′ S, 149° 56′ W

Captain Cook's Polynesia

THE ENGLISHMAN JAMES COOK may well have been, in the 18th century, the world's greatest explorer. Between 1768 and 1779 he led three long seafaring expeditions to the Pacific Ocean, at first in search of the fabled "southern continent" and then of the equally storied Northwest Passage, a shipping route over the top of the world. He visited Tahiti several times, explored New Zealand, mapped the east coast of Australia, crossed the Antarctic Circle, found Hawaii and determined that there was no Northwest Passage. Beyond these accomplishments, he brought back to the western world a better understanding and appreciation of the Pacific's Polynesian people. He learned the rudiments of their language, and during his decade-long exploration of several island groups in the South Pacific became aware of how the Polynesians navigated over vast stretches of ocean in canoes. It is true that Cook was killed by the native Polynesians of Hawaii on his third voyage, but elsewhere in the Pacific, there are places named in his honor, such as the Cook Islands and, here, Cook's Bay in Moorea. To travel in his wake is to take a voyage of discovery all your own, with fabulous scenery and beaches, to boot.

3

Jerusalem

CRUCIAL IN THE HISTORIES of the world's three great monotheistic religions—Judaism, Christianity and Islam—Jerusalem is the city in Israel where Solomon built the first temple, where Jesus went to meet his fate and from which Muhammad ascended to heaven at the end of his night journey. Pilgrims make their way to the Temple Mount and the Western Wall, to the Garden of Gethsemane and the churches of St. Mary Magdalene (above) and of the Holy Sepulchre, to the al-Aqsa Mosque and the Dome of the Rock (above, right), which was completed circa 692 and is the oldest extant Muslim shrine in the world. To quote from Jeremiah 3:17: "They shall call Jerusalem the throne of the Lord; and all the nations shall be gathered unto it, to the name of the Lord, to Jerusalem." Anyone at all interested in religious history—or seeking to bolster his or her own faith in an especially resonant way—should gather unto Jerusalem.

49° 22' N, 0° 52' W

Normandy's Beaches

MOST OF THE BEACHES we have visited in this book have been about fun and sun and surf. Not so the beaches of Normandy, in northern France. They are about what happened here on June 6, 1944: an invasion that altered the course of world history and helped to preserve our freedom. We speak, of course, of World War II's D-Day, the carefully planned assault to liberate northwest Europe. The Normandy beaches were chosen for the attack because they lay within range of air cover and were somewhat less heavily defended by Axis forces than were other places on the French coast. Well before dawn on June 6, a flotilla of six Allied divisions—three U.S., two British, one Canadian and Free French commandos—was already passing across the English Channel. The forces stormed ashore at Sword Beach, Juno Beach, Gold Beach, Omaha Beach, Pointe du Hoc (below, still cratered by bombardment all these decades later) and Utah Beach, suffering heavy casualties but making headway inch by inch. Ultimately, the D-Day invasion would start a march across Europe to Berlin and would mark the beginning of the end for Adolph Hitler's dream of world domination. The beaches are easily found via signs bearing their invasion code names. There are cemeteries stretching to the horizon throughout the area, as well as many memorials and several museums. Inevitably, a visit here is a moving experience for any and all.

JOANNA B. PINNEO/AURORA

31° 47' N, 35° 13' E

PIERRE BOULAT/AURORA

Cape Town

A CITY BEAUTIFUL to behold, Cape Town also bears reminders of the ugly racial strife that has informed it for centuries. It was founded not by natives but by whites when, in 1652, the Dutchman Jan van Riebeeck established the first permanent settlement by Europeans in South Africa. His intention was to sell produce and supplies to ships rounding the southern tip of Africa on trading routes. His nascent colony was soon battling the local Khoi in the first of many confrontations that would be won by the whites. At the other end of Cape Town's history, the long apartheid battles of the 20th century led, finally, to South African democracy in 1994. Van Riebeeck was the first to use offshore Robben Island as a place of banishment, in 1657, and three centuries later it was there that Nelson Mandela was imprisoned. The former penitentiary is now a museum, and an emotional day's journey would include a visit to Mandela's cell, then a walk to Cape Town's City Hall, where, from the balcony on February 11, 1990, he delivered a speech about his homeland hours after being freed.

33° 55′ S, 18° 22′ W ●

Crete

MUCH OF WHAT we in the Western world think and feel today began here. In the centuries circa 2000 to 1450 B.C., Crete was the center of the Minoan culture, which was the oldest form of Greek—and therefore European— civilization. A mountainous island in the eastern Mediterranean with fertile plateaus, Crete provided the Minoans with a suitable setting to grow their sophisticated society. The finest palaces in the world rose here, and the finest frescoes were produced. Many relics of that ancient age are on display at the Minoan archaeological sites of Knossos and Phaistos. Crete was ruled, subsequently, by the Romans, Byzantines, Venetians and Ottoman Turks before becoming part of the modern Greek state, and elsewhere on the large island are excavated sites and buildings from these later periods. Beyond being fascinating for its history, Crete, with its scenic beauty (below, the harbor at Rethymnon) and temperate climate, is altogether delightful.

GEORGE GRIGORIOU/GETTY

Cairo

EGYPT'S "TRIUMPHANT CITY" is one of the world's largest urban areas, and as such features entertaining nightlife, deluxe accommodations and many cultural attractions. As with Jerusalem, there are Islamic, Christian and Jewish monuments and temples to be visited. But when many of us think of Cairo, we think of the legendary antiquities of the Pharaonic era. Chief among these, just outside of town, is the Great Pyramid of Khufu, the only survivor of the original Seven Wonders of the World. Khufu (circa 2551–2528 B.C.; also known as Cheops or Suphis) ruled for two dozen years during the Fourth Dynasty (2574–2465 B.C.) and was reputed to have been quite a tyrant. More than 4,500 years ago he ordered this monumental tomb built (by a work force of 100,000 men) to accommodate none but himself. The pyramid's 2,300,000 blocks of stone, averaging 2.5 tons apiece, eventually climbed to a height of 481 feet; for more than 43 centuries, the Great Pyramid was the tallest building on earth. There are other terrific structures in the realm of Khufu's pyramid on the Giza plain, all installed between 2500 and 2400 B.C. Two other gargantuan pyramids contain the tombs of subsequent kings; in the shadows of the three tremendous constructs are smaller but grand pyramids containing the tombs of several of their queens and, perhaps, that of Khufu's mother, Hetepheres. Lying serenely nearby is the Great Sphinx.

St Andrews

EVEN FROM HERE, behind this printed page, we can see you limbering up that swing. But this is not about the golf. The golf is plenty old and hallowed in St Andrews, to be sure, but St Andrews itself is older and more hallowed still. The big surprise for many American tour groups blowing through for a quick round on the Old Course is that, at its core, this is a college town, on a par (pardon the pun) with Oxford or either of the Cambridges (U.K. or U.S.), and it is also (or at least was) a town of great religious significance. From the Middle Ages until the Reformation, St Andrews was the spiritual capital of Scotland—it was Scotland's Canterbury, Scotland's Rome. The great cathedral, at one time the nation's largest building, is now in ruins—impressive ruins, as we see here, that are well worth walking. Climb St Rule's Tower, and overlook the town sweeping down to the golf links and the shore. The University of St Andrews, Scotland's oldest, dates to 1411. The "modern" university, which consists of Jacobean buildings more than a century and a half old, flows throughout town. Prince William, among many others, studied here recently (he graduated in 2005). And Tiger played golf here. So should you, as a reward after your history lesson.

56°3'N, 2°72'W

21° 2′ N, 156° 98′ W

The Kalaupapa Peninsula

AT ONE TIME FOR MANY PEOPLE, this heavenly place was hell. The first tragedy to occur on the remote five-square-mile peninsula jutting from the north shore of Hawaii's Molokai happened between 1865 and 1895. In those years, the indigenous people were forcibly removed, and in their place, beginning in 1866 and for more than a century, lived sick people—forced into isolation by the authorities. The spread of Hansen's disease, also known as leprosy, had terrified Hawaiian officials who, in their panic, resorted to this most cruel solution. Ah, but there is a hero to this saga: Father Damien, a Catholic priest from Belgium, who arrived at the leper colony in 1873 to offer the inmate patients what physical and religious comfort he could. He contracted the disease himself and died in 1889; the church he led here, St. Philomena, can be visited today. But there are only three ways to access the Kalaupapa Peninsula—by mule, by foot or by small plane. The Molokai Mule Ride is the most popular and, certainly, the most appropriately exotic. As you travel slowly down 1,786 feet of one of the highest sea cliffs in the world on a three-mile trail with 26 switchbacks, you have ample time to be awed by the natural beauty surrounding you, and to contemplate, in perhaps a spiritual way, the sadness that was once pervasive in this heaven on earth.

The Freedom Trail

BOSTON IS A CITY OF multiple charms and attractions. We would certainly urge you to pay a visit to Fenway Park to see the Red Sox play or ride on the Swan Boats in the Public Garden or splash into the Charles River on a Duck Boat Tour or enjoy a prime rib dinner at Durgin-Park. Those are all very fine, and if you get the chance to sample them, please do. But everyone with the means should one day walk the clearly demarcated (in red brick) Freedom Trail. The buildings and streets in Boston, a city known as "The Cradle of Liberty," are, for the most part, quite near one another, and when you visit them during this 2.5-mile walk, you get a palpable sense of the tensions that brewed here in the early 1770s. Those tensions led to the Boston Tea Party and, finally, to the Shot Heard Round the World, which was fired in Concord on April 19, 1775, igniting the Revolutionary War. Faneuil Hall, where the rebels Hancock, Adams and company used to gather as a cabal, is part of the 16-site trail, as are the Old South Meeting House (below) and the Old North Church, where two lanterns once flashed warning that the British were coming by sea. Paul Revere mounted his horse that night, and shouted the news to colonials throughout the countryside. Minutemen poured forth to Lexington and Concord—and so, we started on the road to becoming the nation we are today.

DAVID MUENCH/CORBIS

KEVIN FLEMING/CORBIS

Antietam

SEPTEMBER 17, 1862, was the bloodiest day in American history, bar none. At the Battle of Antietam in Maryland, 23,000 soldiers from the Union and Confederate armies were killed or wounded in 12 vicious hours. Consider: D-Day saw approximately one-ninth as many U.S. casualties. The encounter was, as might well be imagined, a crucial one in the course of the Civil War. Eighteen days earlier, Robert E. Lee's Confederate Army of Northern Virginia had prevailed at Second Manassas and was poised to invade the North for the first time. When it did so, George McClellan's Army of the Potomac, which greatly outnumbered Lee's force, moved to intercept. They met at Antietam Creek in Sharpsburg (above, Burnside Bridge, a site of fierce fighting). The North suffered somewhat heavier losses but carried the day when Lee was forced to retreat. The narrow strategic win had great consequences: The South had hoped a victory would prompt either England or France to lend support to its effort; now that wouldn't be forthcoming. And President Abraham Lincoln was emboldened to abolish slavery in the South by issuing a preliminary Emancipation Proclamation, making whatever remained of the war a clear moral crusade. The National Battlefield at Antietam allows visitors to return to the scene of courage and carnage. Take a self-guided hike on any of the trails—Cornfield, Final Attack, Union Advance, Antietam Remembered, Sherrick Farm, Snavely Ford—and just...*imagine*.

Vietnam

THE NATIONAL TOURIST BOARD will tell you about new resorts near the beaches and will present statistics proving a sizeable uptick in vacationers coming to Vietnam for rest and relaxation. They are vying—or hope to vie—with Thailand for the sun-and-sand trade in Southeast Asia. But for Americans visiting Vietnam, the implications of our shared past with this land are inescapable, whether we like it or not. Many people do want to confront that past, and you can find tours of the exotic country that are specific to Vietnam War history. Some of these are targeted narrowly at veterans of the conflict, but most of them are for people interested in living history. Any Vietnam visit will include Ho Chi Minh City, formerly Saigon, and memories will surely flood back of frantic helicopter flights from downtown rooftops. Today, you can crawl, flashlight in hand, through the Cu Chi tunnels, which were used by the Viet Cong when Saigon was attacked during the Tet Offensive. You can travel deep into the Mekong Delta (seen here), where, once, Swift Boats ventured. It is useful for an American to visit memorials at Da Nang, Chu Lai and even at the site of the My Lai Massacre. Meantime, there is everywhere the present-day peace and tropical lushness of Vietnam—all grown back.

10° 19' N, 106° 40' E

The Dinosaurs of Wyoming

THERE ARE TRULY IMPRESSIVE mounted dinosaur skeletons at fine science museums throughout the land. But in Wyoming you can get up close and personal with the bygone beasties at several dig sites open to the public. The one seen here is on federal land near Greybull, where excavations have yielded 12 large Jurassic Era sauropods, including one of the world's largest allosauruses, since 1934. An hour's drive south in Thermopolis is the Wyoming Dinosaur Center, which has more than 60 dig sites in a 500-acre area. In one hole are the remains of several more allosauruses; in another, easily discernible tracks; in a third, an apatosaurus (formerly known as brontosaurus). In the museum gallery, there are 28 more skeletons, the star of which is a 106-foot-long, well-named supersaurus. Wyoming, an altogether more welcoming place these days than it was when this big fella roamed the range, allows you to not only contemplate the size of dinosaurs but to actually picture them dominating the landscape about you.

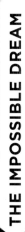

_OUKAS HAPSIS/AUROFA

Lost Atlantis

WHAT MAKES THIS ONE IMPOSSIBLE IS: You're never going to be sure you're right, not unless you can get in touch with Plato and ask him. It was the great philosopher who, n 360 B.C., first told the story of an idyllic island civilization that was destroyec by an earthquake or a tsunami. A not dissimilar fate—death by volcano—had befallen the Greek island of Santorini (left) centuries earlier, and many have speculated that this was the model for Atlantis. Others have "found" Atlantis in or around Cuba, including on the plains of Pinar del Rio (opposite, bottom). Still others have said that the frozen continent Antarctica (below) is the true location of the lost continent. There are scores of nominees, from Andalusia to New Zealand, and of only one thing can we be certain: A quest in search of Atlantis would take the seeker to some truly wondrous lands.

Wildflower Hall

IN JAMES HILTON'S 1933 novel *Lost Horizon* and in the Frank Capra film version of the book, Shangri-La is a mystical realm in the Kunlun Mountains in east-central Asia—a quiet place, hidden from the outside world, where the inhabitants are content, calm and extraordinarily long-lived. Many tourism campaigns in the Himalayan region have sought to trade on the allure of Shangri-La, even unto an effort by three separate tourist boards to pool their efforts in a single, focused Shangri-La assault. Wildflower Hall was not part of that initiative, but certainly does its best to approximate Shangri-La here in the real world. Once the estate of Lord Kitchener, who was commander of British troops in India from 1902 to 1909, it is now a luxury hotel and spa perched at 8,350 feet on a knoll in India's Himalayas. There are wondrous views from all rooms, and the outdoor Jacuzzi is perhaps the world's most decadent place for enjoying a light winter snowstorm. The spa offers holistic treatments based on Ayurvedic, Asian and Western therapies; a walk in the woods—the hotel is surrounded by 23 acres of virgin cedar and pine—is equally rejuvenating. If this isn't Shangri-La, nothing is.

31° 13' N, 77° 23' E

The Camargue

WHAT IS, ESSENTIALLY, a wetlands is put forth here as a place of romance. Really? Ah, *mais oui*. France can make almost anything romantic, and it is so with the Camargue, an immense, flat expanse at the delta of the Rhône River. Go in the spring, for in the summer it is too hot and infested with irritating insects and the tourist hordes, and in the winter it is too windy and drear. In spring the wildflowers are out, and the nearby towns of Arles and Saintes-Maries-de-la-Mer are yours for the enjoying. After a lovely night's rest at an inn, make your way out to the extraordinary shore by the Mediterranean. Venture near the 16,600-acre saltwater lagoon Étang de Vaccarès, a protected zoological and botanical reserve. There, you'll see herring gulls, black-headed gulls and the feature attraction, hundreds of pink flamingoes. In the reserve dwell not only native black bulls but the famous white horses of Camargue. They are ponies, actually, and only develop their signature white coat at age five or six (below, young and old). If you're lucky, you and yours will spy one in the fen. *Très romantique.*

HENRY AUSLOOS/PETER ARNOLD INC.

Kyoto

IT WAS THE CAPITAL of imperial Japan for more than a millennium, from 794 to 1868, and has long been regarded as the center of Japanese culture, religion and . . . gardening. This last item is not to be slighted; it is a craft that has been raised to a true art form in Japan and the esteemed and lovely Kyoto, home to close to 1.5 million people, is known in Japan as a "garden city." Another way to think of it is as the country's center of Zen, and with 2,000 temples and shrines, an air of tranquility pervades the place. Do visit the Arashiyama district just outside the urban center. Walk the ages-old Togetsukyo Bridge, and gaze upon Mount Arashi. Take a boat tour in the Hozu River through a wooded valley or a trip on the aptly named Sagano Romantic Train. Then repair to one of Kyoto's large or small hotels. For the well-heeled, perhaps this will be to the Tawaraya Ryokan. You don't feel, here, as though you're checking in—but visiting friends. Your room has futons and a soaking tub; some rooms open onto private gardens. It may just be the world's most peaceful hostelry.

The Cinque Terre

THE NAMES OF THE VILLAGES are lovely on the tongue, to the ear or on the page: Riomaggiore, Manarola, Corniglia, Vernazza (seen here) and Monterosso al Mare. As the last implies, they are on the sea—specifically, on the rocky Mediterranean coastline of La Spezia province, in northwest Italy's Liguria region. (More wonderful words!) A train running between La Spezia and Genoa connects the five, but there are also walking trails (steep in places) from village to village; a stretch from Manarola to Riomaggiore says it all in its name, Via dell'Amore, or Lovers' Walk. There are flowers everywhere throughout the Cinque Terre, and olives and grapes grow in the hills above the towns. These are ancient villages, and the coziest lodging is to be had at the many bed-and-breakfasts. In summer, you can swim in the small inlets Palaedo and Marina, and in the evenings relax on the balcony of your apartment or at a cliff-top cafe, with a glass of crisp, locally made white wine. Holding hands, you listen to the music made by the Mediterranean.

44° 6′ N, 9° 44′ E

Montréal

IT'S TIME TO RETURN TO Canada's fabled city of romance. Years ago, this charmed and charming French-flavored metropolis was at the very top of any American couple's list of easy-to-visit cities that offered at least a soupçon (or considerably more) of foreign flair. But then the powerful Quebec separatist movement forced Montréal to get in line—a hard line—against all things Anglo, and business and tourism fled to Toronto, Vancouver and other places. The city has since moderated its radical stance (evidence: The IMAX movies in the Vieux-Port area run in English as well as French). There is no longer an automatic anti-English or anti-American hostility. The city is, as far as the American tourist is concerned, back. The Vieux-Port (or old port, below) is just as you remember it: bright, full of energy, fascinating by day, festive at night. The Notre-Dame Basilica is every bit as magnificent as you recall. The accommodations at the Ritz-Carlton or the Queen Elizabeth are as sumptuous as ever. Depending on your views of hipness, you might ask for suite 1742 in the Queen Liz. That's where the recently wed John and Yoko (Monsieur Lennon and Madame Ono) held one of their wacky, semi-notorious bed-ins for peace in 1969. History and love: That has forever been Montréal.

DALLAS AND JOHN HEATON/AURORA

YVES MARCOUX/GETTY

Brussels

THIS BELGIAN CITY OF A MILLION CITIZENS is cosmopolitan and sophisticated—it has two official languages, Dutch and French, and everyone seems to speak English, too—but it is also intimate, friendly and warm-hearted. Brussels is an old town laced with meandering cobblestone lanes and countless small shops selling chocolates, pastries and antiques; and there's a daily flea market selling almost everything. Somehow, miraculously, it seems that all pathways lead to the large courtyard of the Grand Place (above), one of the most splendid open-air plazas to be found anywhere in Europe. In the courtyard, you can while away the hours at one of several cafes whose umbrellas bloom in the morning sun. For breakfast there are waffles, of course, and in midafternoon there is no better repast that an order of moules frites (mussels with the best french fries you've ever tasted). To accompany, ask for a luscious beer crafted in the countryside by Trappist monks. Work off your meal with a late-afternoon walk in the Sonian Forest (it's right outside town), and then retire to your luxury hotel or small bed-and-breakfast. You will fall asleep with a smile on your face after a day in gentle Brussels.

Saint Lucia

ONE OF THE WINDWARD ISLANDS in the eastern Caribbean Sea, Saint Lucia has bopped back and forth between British and French rule for centuries but is today its own nation. Twenty-seven miles long and 14 wide, Saint Lucia is small but its topography is varied. It is a volcanic island with mountains rising to nearly 3,000 feet, and in the interior there are lush rainforests accented by wild orchids, where parrots and birds of paradise thrive. The beaches are shaded by large palm trees; it has been said that Saint Lucia seems like a tropical isle from the South Pacific that has been picked up and plunked in the Caribbean. Cruise lines arrive regularly, as do lovers. Saint Lucia, which guarantees a sensational wedding album, hosts thousands of nuptial ceremonies each year. And the celebrants usually stay for the honeymoon.

Napa Valley

GETTING THERE IS HALF THE FUN. Your trip to Napa may include San Francisco, romantic in its own right, and the hour's drive north from there becomes ever more glorious as the miles pass. Do stop in Sonoma County, where California's viticulture originated. And then on to Napa. In the valley's half-dozen towns, you have myriad choices of places to stay: bed-and-breakfasts, inns and spas with natural hot springs, and for dining, some of the finest restaurants in the region. Napa's scenery is itself a feast for the eyes in a state whose variety of scenic splendor is extraordinary. If you intend a serious wine tour, it is best to arrange times in advance with the smaller, family-owned wineries. There's a good chance the vintner will show you around, explaining the craft, the vintages—the magic of wine.

MICHAEL MELFORD

The Inn at Little Washington

SIXTY-SEVEN MILES WEST OF WASHINGTON, D.C., nestled between the Blue Ridge Mountains and the Shenandoah Valley, is a tiny village that was the first place in the land to be named for George Washington. Not much has changed in this region since a young George surveyed the countryside. In 1899, a local carpenter built a handsome white house, and that renovated building is now part of the celebrated country inn. The man behind the Inn at Little Washington is master chef Patrick O'Connell, whose refined American cuisine is served nightly in peak season. There are 18 guest rooms, each of them supremely inviting and whimsically decorated. The tone of the inn—a combination of classicism, luxury and sporty fun—is set when you arrive to be met by a smiling bellman trailed by the inn's Dalmatian wearing a string of pearls (the dog has the pearls, not the bellman). There isn't a lot to do in Little Washington but relax, renew, have a cocktail and, above all, partake of possibly the best meal you've ever had. The inn's grace notes come with a price tag, but for a special romantic occasion, nothing can top a stay here.

Lake Wanaka

NEARLY A THOUSAND FEET ABOVE SEA LEVEL, in the center of New Zealand's gorgeous South Island, lies this 27-mile-long, more than 1,000-foot-deep lake—one of the world's most beautiful. To the north are mountains, big ones that rise up to 6,000 feet above sea level. The lakeside town, a charming place to stay, also goes by the name Wanaka. Sheep farms dot the surrounding countryside; it has often been said that the South Island has more sheep than humans on its census rolls, and no visitor to this high-country region, where scores of sheep stations were established in the 19th century, would doubt it. Another, more recent occupation here is the making of wine; the pinot noirs, in particular, are delicious. This secret gem's extraordinary allure was used in *Mission Impossible III* when "Lake Wanaka" was given as the coded answer to a crucial question of the hero, played by Tom Cruise. It let him identify his wife, for Wanaka was a cherished place for the two of them. Now that's romance.

Seville

Don Juan's earliest seductions were perpetrated in this passionate town—enough said. Columbus also started from a nearby port on a far different type of conquest. And it was here that Georges Bizet's Carmen couldn't choose between her army officer and her bullfighter; on opera stages around the world, she reenacts her torment regularly. Seville wears its heart on its sleeve, and that is all to the good for visitors to this hot (especially in summer) Spanish city. The nightlife is sensational; it never ends until the sun says it must. In the daytime, if it is your wont, take in a bullfight. You are in the warm heart of Andalusia here, and cultural signatures are the bullring ballet and flamenco music. You don't have to get up and join the dance, but simply to watch gives immense pleasure. Seville is a fascinating city to look at—800 years of Moorish occupation are everywhere evident—but it is even more thrilling as a feeling, a vibe.

GLEN ALLISON/MIRA

Madeira Island

In 1938, a short documentary was made about the place: *Madeira: 'Isle of Romance.'* Seven decades later, the appelation still applies, and, in fact, so little has changed that much of the same footage would be useable today. The largest in a group of islands that form an archipelago in the Atlantic Ocean off the coast of both Europe and Africa, Madeira is a lovely, slow-moving place. Although it sits upon the African tectonic plate, it belongs to Portugal and reflects that culture in its daily life. While the living is luxurious at the famous Reid's Palace hotel in Funchal, the island is calm and pretty and laid-back. It is almost precisely the size of Saint Lucia, and its mountains reach even higher—to over 4,000 feet in many places (Pico Ruivo tops out at 6,107 feet). With the Gulf Stream running this way, the climate is temperate. It is a land of tropical flowers and fruits ... and yes, the famed Madeira wine comes from here. The island has a loyal clientele and is a regular stopping-off point for cruise lines, but it has not yet been redis-covered as the world-beating isle of romance it is. That's up to you.

GERALD BRIMACOMBE

Burgh Island

WE RETURN TO ENGLAND A FINAL TIME, to a tidal island off the coast of Devon where Britons of the 5th century used to revel on Bigbury Beach. Subsequently, this island in the English Channel became home to monks, who quieted things down. (Well, they did brew mead, which went down well with the local fishermen.) Smugglers and other sorts of pirates were frequent on the island in the 18th century, but in 1895, an enterprise began that would point toward the present day. Music hall singer George Chirgwin built a hotel, and several generations later, that building was replaced by the white art deco Burgh Island Hotel, a grand and special place that dominates the island experience, which is: luxury, calm, romance, peace. In other words, all that one could ever ask of a place.

JASON HAWKES/CORBIS

Whidbey Island

THE ISLANDS OF THE PACIFIC NORTHWEST, including the famous San Juans, are notable for their rough, rustic, rare beauty. Too often overlooked is Whidbey Island, one of nine in Washington State's Island County, lying about 30 miles north of Seattle at the northern boundary of Puget Sound. Perhaps this is because Whidbey is bigger (about 50 miles long) and more populous (nearly 60,000 residents, though half of them are scattered throughout the countryside) than the others. Or perhaps it's because of the Naval Air Station that dominates Whidbey's northern end. But we are talking of Whidbey Island south of Oak Harbor. Here, the villages of Langley and Coupeville are serene, and the landscape is lovely; large Douglas firs and big-leaf maples surround you. If you're inclined to reread *Snow Falling on Cedars,* this is the vacation for it. Whidbey is big and hearty, like the other islands in the sound, and, in its southern half, very special.

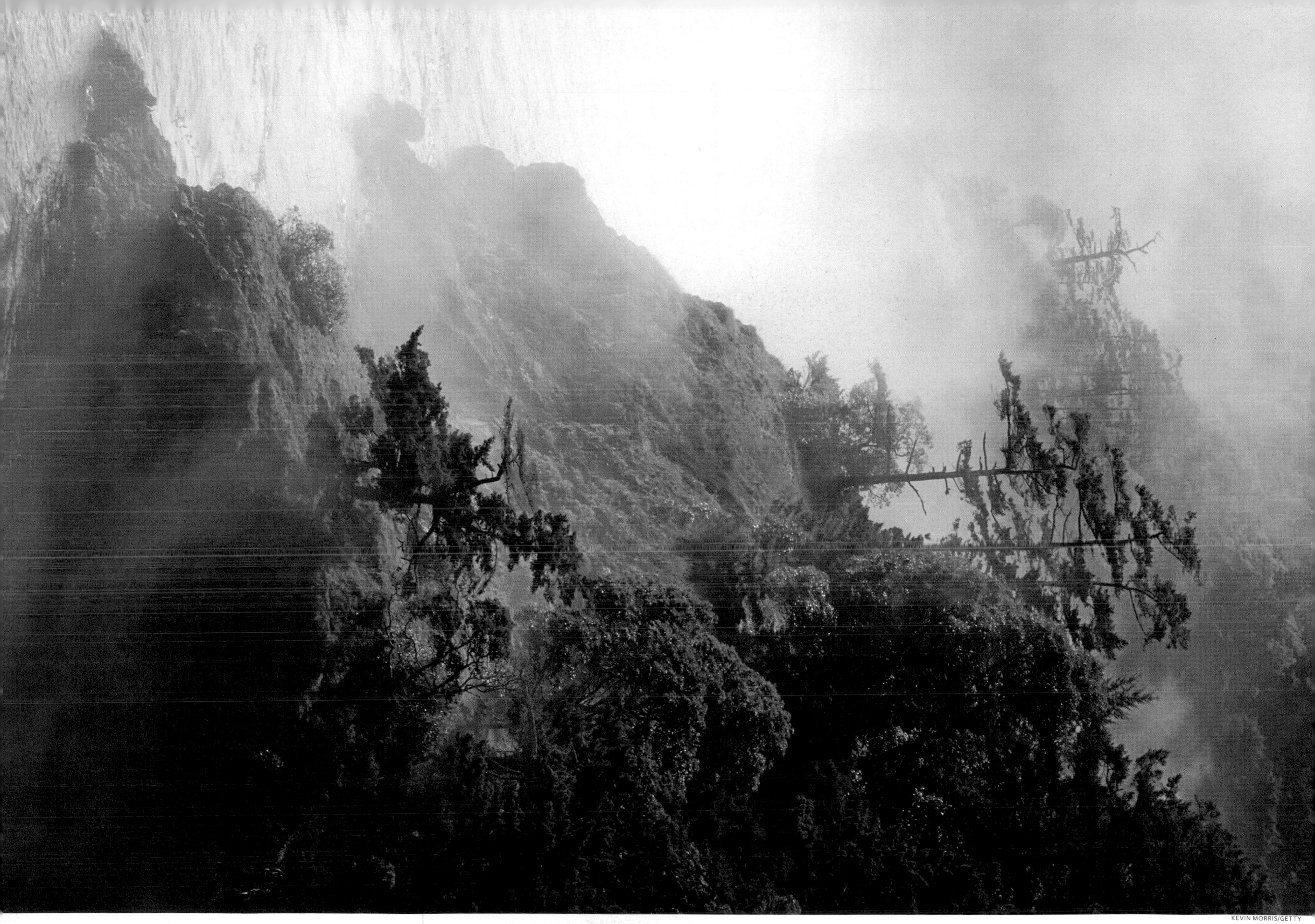

48°21'N, 122°39'W

KEVIN MORRIS/GETTY

44° 33′ N, 74° 13′ W

The Point

THE SIGN SAYS NO VISITORS, but it doesn't really mean it. In fact, it wants visitors (if they've brought a well-oiled checkbook). The Point, a New York state Adirondack Great Camp, one of the most splendiferous of them all and built by a bona fide member of the Rockefeller family, is now a super-luxury resort—open to you, should you have the dough. Once you've made your reservation, you fly into the airport at Saranac Lake, drive 20 minutes, veer onto an unmarked road and proceed down the wooded peninsula until you reach … *The Point*. Unbeatable canoeing and kayaking, walking and hiking await. And eating: Three gourmet meals a day come with the tariff, as does absolute seclusion and serenity. Which is not to say The Point doesn't hop. On Wednesday and Saturday nights, black tie is recommended for the gents. The pub pours till dawn, at which hour you retreat to your room to find the fire already burning. Children are not allowed at The Point. It is for romantic couples, away from it all.

Kennedy Cottage

WHERE DO THE PEOPLE who can honeymoon anywhere choose to honeymoon? Some go to a private island, some never leave the yacht. We look back here to the romance of the American Camelot and ask: Where did Jack and Jackie go? First to Acapulco and then to California, to this boutique resort in Montecito called the San Ysidro Ranch (left). A lodging since 1893, the ranch was turned into a Hollywood hide-away of choice by the actor Ronald Colman in the 1930s. Ever since, it's been about romance: Vivien Leigh and Laurence Olivier were married here, and more recently, it has been reported that stars such as Julia Roberts and Danny Moder and J.Lo and Marc Anthony honeymooned here. The newlywed Kennedys did, in 1953, in a cottage on the grounds now named in their honor (below). It's yours—for only $2,995 a night.

Off We Go!

If you require any further inspiration to get up out of that easy chair and flee to your dream destination, allow this soaring impala in Kenya's Masai Mara preserve to supply it. Bon voyage!

NORTH AMERICA